OFFICIAL GUIDE

TO THE

Yellowstone National Park.

A MANUAL FOR TOURISTS,

Containing a description of the Mammoth Hot Springs, the Geyser Basins, the Cataracts, the Canons, and other features of the

NEW WONDERLAND,

WITH NINETEEN ILLUSTRATIONS.

AND

AN APPENDIX,

Containing Rates for Special Conveyances, as well as Other Miscellaneous Information.

W. C. RILEY, PUBLISHER, ST. PAUL, MINN.

1890.

Copyright, 1890, by *W. C. Riley*,
St. Paul, Minn.

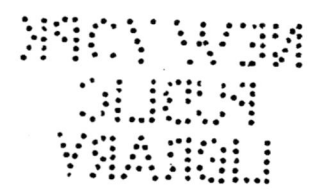

BROWN, TREACY & CO.,
PRINTERS AND BLANK BOOK MANUFACTURERS,
ST. PAUL, MINN.

This scarce antiquarian book is included in our special *Legacy Reprint Series*. In the interest of creating a more extensive selection of rare historical book reprints, we have chosen to reproduce this title even though it may possibly have occasional imperfections such as missing and blurred pages, missing text, poor pictures, markings, dark backgrounds and other reproduction issues beyond our control. Because this work is culturally important, we have made it available as a part of our commitment to protecting, preserving and promoting the world's literature. Thank you for your understanding.

CONTENTS.

	PAGES.
RULES AND REGULATIONS OF YELLOWSTONE NATIONAL PARK,	6
YELLOWSTONE NATIONAL PARK—HISTORY AND EXPLORATION,	9–17
THE UPPER YELLOWSTONE VALLEY,	18–25
THE MAMMOTH HOT SPRINGS,	26–36
GRAND TOUR OF THE PARK,	37
Obsidian Cliffs,	39–41
Norris Geyser Basin,	41–44
Virginia Cañon Road,	45
Yellowstone River,	47
Upper Falls of the Yellowstone River,	47–49
Lower Falls of the Yellowstone River,	49–52
Grand Cañon,	52–59
Crater Hills,	60–63
Yellowstone Lake,	67–76
Lower Geyser Basin,	78–84
Midway Geyser Basin,	85–89
Upper Geyser Basin,	91–112
Shoshone Lake and Kepler's Cascades,	113, 115
Mount Schurz and Monument Geyser Basin,	118
Mount Washburn and Tower Falls,	121–126
FOSSIL FORESTS AND HOODOO COUNTRY,	127–130
FAUNA OF THE PARK,	131–132
FLORA OF THE PARK,	133–134
APPENDIX,	135–140
Distances between Points of Interest,	135
Elevations in National Park,	136
The Climate of the National Park,	137
Temperature of the Geysers and Hot Springs,	138
Bunsen's Theory of Geyser Formation and Action,	138, 139
Rates for Special Conveyances in Yellowstone Park,	140

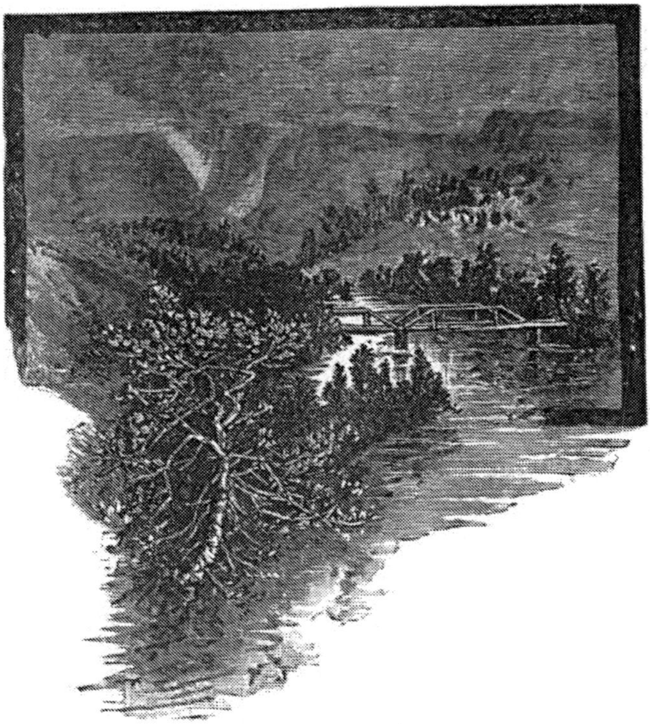

ILLUSTRATIONS.

From Sketches by A. von Schilling *and Photographs by* F. J. Haynes.
Engraved by E. Heinemann *and* A. Demarest.

	PAGE.
Yellowstone River,	4
Gate of the Mountains, near Livingston,	7
Through the Lower Cañon of the Yellowstone,	11
General View of Gardiner River Valley and Hot Springs,	27
Mammoth Hot Spring Terraces,	30
Lake of the Woods and Obsidian Cliffs,	38
Norris Geyser Basin—Monarch Geyser in Action,	42
Upper Falls of the Yellowstone River,	46
Great Falls of the Yellowstone River,	50
Crater Hills, Mud Geyser, and Hot Springs on Yellowstone Lake,	53
Views in Grand Cañon,	66
Yellowstone Lake,	70
Old Faithful Geyser in Eruption,	94
General View Upper Geyser Basin,	97
Bee Hive Geyser in Eruption,	99
Giant Geyser in Eruption,	107
Kepler's Cascades,	114
Gibbon Falls,	117
Monument Geyser Basin,	120
Tower Falls,	122

RULES AND REGULATIONS

OF THE

Yellowstone National Park.

DEPARTMENT OF THE INTERIOR,
WASHINGTON, July 1, 1888.

1. It is forbidden to remove or injure the sediments or incrustations around the geysers, hot springs, or steam vents; or to deface the same by written inscription or otherwise; or to throw any substance into the springs or geyser vents; or to injure or disturb in any manner, any of the mineral deposits, natural curiosities or wonders within the Park.

2. It is forbidden to ride or drive upon any of the geyser or hot spring formations, or to turn loose stock to graze in their vicinity.

3. It is forbidden to cut or injure any growing timber. Camping parties will be allowed to use dead or fallen timber for fuel.

4. Fires shall be lighted only when necessary, and completely extinguished when not longer required. The utmost care should be exercised at all times to avoid setting fire to the timber and grass.

5. Hunting, capturing, injuring, or killing any bird or animal within the Park is prohibited. The outfits of persons found hunting, or in possession of game killed in the Park, will be subject to seizure and confiscation.

6. Fishing with nets, seines, traps, or by the use of drugs or explosives, or in any other way than with hook and line, is prohibited. Fishing for purposes of merchandise or profit is forbidden by law.

7. No person will be permitted to reside permanently or to engage in any business in the Park, without permission, in writing, from the Department of the Interior. The Superintendent may grant authority to competent persons to act as guides, and revoke the same at his discretion.

8. No drinking saloon or bar-room will be permitted within the limits of the Park.

9. Private notices or advertisements shall not be posted or displayed within the Park, except such as may be necessary for the convenience and guidance of the public, upon buildings on leased ground.

10. Persons who render themselves obnoxious by disorderly conduct or bad behavior, or who violate any of the foregoing rules, will be summarily removed from the Park, under authority of the Statute setting apart the Park "as a pleasuring ground for the people," and providing that it "shall be under the exclusive control of the Secretary of the Interior, whose duty it shall be to make and publish such rules and regulations as he shall deem necessary or proper," and who "generally shall be authorized to take all such measures as shall be necessary or proper to fully carry out the object and purposes of this act." WM. F. VILAS, Secretary of the Interior.

Gate of the Mountains, near Livingston.

Yellowstone National Park.

THE Yellowstone National Park is situated in the midst of the most elevated part of the erratic Rocky Mountains, and within the shadow of the confused and forbidding peaks by which it is engirdled are born the rills which grow into the mightiest rivers of the United States. From the summit of Mount Washburn, the highest point of observation embraced by the Park, may be seen the grim and towering walls which partition a complex of waters, forcing the flow either eastward, by way of the Gulf of Mexico, into the Atlantic, or westward into the Pacific Ocean.

But the fact that here rise the springs of the Missouri-Mississippi system, as well as those of the Columbia and the Colorado, is lost sight of in view of the far more striking features of this remarkable region. Nowhere else in all the wide world are to be seen, so close to the surface, on so grand and varied a scale, undoubted evidences of existing subterranean fires; nowhere else is the opportunity given to note with ease the lingering death throes of the terrible volcanic forces which convulsed the round world to its very centre in ages long ago.

An area of greater value to the student, and of more interest to the tourist, would be hard to find. It was, therefore, a wise and creditable act of the United States Congress of 1872 to withdraw this portion of the public domain from settlement, and devote it in perpetuity to the use and pleasure of the people as a National Park. This measure stands out the more boldly as an instance of commendable foresight, when it is remembered that it was based upon the report of a single official survey, that of Prof. F. V. Hayden in 1871, made at a time when the country was almost inaccessible, and when a lack of proper interest in the subject might have been antici-

~~pated~~ and excused. But to the zealous advocacy of Prof. Hayden, and to his untiring personal efforts, the favorable action of Congress upon the project was mainly due. The act of dedication was as follows:

Be it enacted by the Senate and House of Representatives of the United States of America in Congress assembled, That the tract of land in the Territories of Montana and Wyoming, lying near the headwaters of the Yellowstone River, and described as follows, to wit: Commencing at the junction of Gardiner's River with the Yellowstone River, and running east to the meridian passing ten miles to the eastward of the most eastern point of Yellowstone Lake; thence south along the said meridian to the parallel of latitude passing ten miles south of the most southern point of Yellowstone Lake; thence west along said parallel to the meridian passing fifteen miles west of the most western point of Madison Lake; thence north along said meridian to the latitude of the junction of the Yellowstone and Gardiner's Rivers; thence east to the place of beginning,—is hereby reserved and withdrawn from settlement, occupancy or sale under the laws of the United States, and dedicated and set apart as a public park or pleasure ground for the benefit and enjoyment of the people; and all persons who shall locate, settle upon or occupy the same or any part thereof, except as hereinafter provided, shall be considered trespassers and removed therefrom.

SEC. 2. That said public park shall be under the exclusive control of the Secretary of the Interior, whose duty it shall be, as soon as practicable, to make and publish such rules and regulations as he may deem necessary or proper for the care and management of the same. Such regulations shall provide for the preservation from injury or spoliation of all timber, mineral deposits, natural curiosities or wonders within said park, and their retention in their natural condition.

AN ACT making appropriation for sundry civil expenses of the Government, for the fiscal year ending June 30, 1884, and for other purposes:

EXTRACT.

The Secretary of the Interior may lease small portions of ground in the park, not exceeding ten acres in extent for each tract, on which may be erected hotels and the necessary out-buildings, and for a period not exceeding ten years; but such lease shall not include any of the geysers or other objects of curiosity or interest in said park, or exclude the public from the free and convenient approach thereto; or include any ground within one quarter of a mile of any of the geysers or the Yellowstone Falls, nor shall there be leased more than ten acres to any one person or corporation; nor shall any hotel or other buildings be erected within the park until such lease shall be executed by the Secretary of the Interior, and all contracts, agreements, or exclusive privileges heretofore made or given in regard to said park, or any part thereof, are hereby declared to be invalid; nor shall the Secretary of the Interior, in any lease which he may make and execute, grant any exclusive privileges within said park, except upon the ground leased. The Secretary of War, upon the request of the Secretary of the Interior, is hereby authorized and directed to make the

Through the Lower Cañon of the Yellowstone River.

necessary detail of troops to prevent trespassers or intruders from entering the park for the purpose of destroying the game or objects of curiosity therein, or for any other purpose prohibited by law, and to remove such persons from the park, if found therein.

Approved March 3d, 1883.

The tract embraced within the National Park limits lies mainly in northwestern Wyoming, including only a narrow strip of southern Montana and eastern Idaho. No general survey having been made, these boundaries do not describe any natural divisions. They include a region which stretches a few miles east of the meridian of 110° west longitude, and about the same distance west of the meridian of 111°, and a few miles north of the parallel of 45°, and not quite so far south as 44° north latitude. These purely arbitrary lines contain an area fifty-five miles in width from east to west, and sixty-five miles in length from north to south, or about 3,575 square miles. This gives an extent about 200 square miles greater than that of the States of Rhode Island and Delaware combined. Most of the territory is situated east of that portion of the main range of the irregular Rocky Mountain chain in which are the sources of the Madison and Gallatin Rivers, the middle and eastern of the three large streams which unite and form the Missouri.

This region is, in reality, less one large park than a group of smaller ones, partially or wholly isolated on both sides of the Continental Divide. The lowest elevation of any of the narrow valleys of the Park is 6,000 feet above the sea, and several of them are from 1,000 to 2,000 feet higher. Mountain ranges, hemming in these valleys on every side, rear their proud peaks from 10,000 to 12,000 feet. Throughout the year the nights are cool, and seldom free from frost; consequently the Park is entirely unsuited to agriculture. Being of volcanic origin, it would be vain to seek for minerals among its rocks. But though this area has been deprived by Nature of the means of supporting a permanent population, it is endowed with features so curious and remarkable that it must always attract large numbers of transient visitors. The Park is a region of wonder, terror and delight. Nature puts forth all her powers, and her moods are ever changing from "grave to gay, from lively to severe." Here tremendous geysers shoot up their mighty fountains, causing the earth to groan and tremble by their violence; countless hot springs, indescribable in their strange beauty, show depths as translucent as the ambient air; pools of seething mud, casting up jets of colored paste, bewilder by their curious activity. And, as if these were not sufficient, here, too, is to be seen the most varied and lavish display of picturesque scenery. The Park unfolds a succession of pictures, each more striking than the other. There are serried, snow-mantled mountains, profound cañons, mighty cataracts, verdant valleys, beautiful woods, sylvan streams, foaming cascades, and mirror-like lakes. The forests abound in noble game, and the waters of the mountain ranges are alive with fish. The glorious air acts as a tonic upon mind and body. Doubtless the numerous mineral springs are full of health-giving properties for the invalid. In short, the Yellowstone National Park is precisely adapted to be the public pleasuring ground for the benefit and enjoyment of the people, which Congress, in 1872, declared it should forever be.

History and Explorations.—The following brief account of the history of the Park and the explorations of the region is taken from the report made to Dr. Hayden by Henry Gannett, E. M., on the geographical field work of the United States Geological Survey during the season of 1878:

"The first authentic information regarding the great natural wonders of the Park was derived from a prospecting party under the leadership of Capt. W. W. DeLacy, who, in 1863, visited the Lower Geyser Basin. Previous to this time it seems that the region was known to but a few hunters and trappers, and their tales were treated as the wildest of romancing, as, indeed, many of them were, the mind of the trapper being singularly prone to exaggeration. The earliest reference to the hot springs is in the stories of a trapper by the name of Colter (or Coulter), who accompanied Lewis and Clarke's celebrated expedition across the continent. On the return of this expedition, when below the mouth of the Yellowstone, Colter was discharged, at his own request, and immediately returned to the country above the forks of the Missouri. In this neighborhood, probably on the Jefferson, his companion, Potts, was killed by Blackfeet, and he was captured. Almost miraculously he escaped from them, and, entirely naked, made his way to a trading post on the Big Horn. After this he lived for a year or more among the Bannacks, whose range included what is now the Yellowstone Park. Either during his perilous journey, after his escape from the Blackfeet, or during his sojourn among the Bannacks, he became acquainted with the region of the hot springs and geysers, for we find him in Missouri, in 1810, telling marvelous tales of lakes of burning pitch, of land on fire, hot springs and geysers. His stories were, of course, treated as travelers' tales, and "Colter's Hell" was classed with Lilliput, Symmes' Hole, and other inventions of overdeveloped imaginations.

"Later we find the knowledge of this country more generally diffused among this people. Colonel Raynolds, in his report on the 'Exploration of the Yellowstone,' in 1859–60, refers to 'some of these Munchausen tales' as follows (p. 77):

"'One was to this effect: In many parts of the country petrifactions and fossils are very numerous, and, as a consequence, it was claimed that in some locality (I was not able to fix it definitely) a large tract of sage is perfectly petrified, with all the leaves and branches in perfect condition, the general appearance of the plain being *unlike* (like?) that of the rest of the country; *but all is stone;* while the rabbits, sage hens and other animals usually found in such localities are still there, perfectly petrified, and as natural as when they were living; and, more wonderful still, the petrified bushes bear the most wonderful fruit; diamonds, rubies, sapphires, emeralds, etc., etc., as large as black walnuts, are found in abundance.'

"This story, absurd as it sounds, has a large basis in fact. The narrator, however, had mixed up distinct phenomena, and over all had spread lavishly the coloring of his imagination. There are fields of sage, as well as bits of forest, which, lying in immediate proximity to groups of springs, have been petrified while standing. The hot, silicious water from the springs is drawn up through the pores of the wood, and between the wood and the bark, by capillary attraction, and, depositing silica wherever it goes, the tree or bush is rapidly transformed into rock.

"The story of the remarkable fruit borne by these stone trees is not far from correct, the main difference between the story and the fact being that the fruit is borne on the outside and inside of the trunks of the trees, instead of on the ends of the branches. The mineral species are not as given in the story, either; but that is a matter of no vital importance. In the process of silicification of wood, the last result of all is the production of quartz crystals. The tree trunk is converted totally into crystalline quartz, radiating from within outward, the crystals being all crowded out of shape. The inside and outside of the hollow cylinder of quartz, which represents the former tree, are covered with the characteristic quartz pyramids. Such products of silicification are very abundant in the Park, particularly on Amethyst Ridge, and are, undoubtedly, the 'stone fruit' of the petrified trees and bushes. The crystals are colorless, amethystine or yellow, and, according to the color, are known to the mountain man as diamond, amethyst, topaz, etc. It is unnecessary to say that the part of the story relating to animal life was manufactured from whole cloth.

"Many other legends had long been current among mountain men, some of which are briefly referred to in Colonel Norris' report to the Secretary of the Interior for 1878; but none of them seem to have attracted any attention. That white men have been in the Park, prior to any printed record, is evidenced by the discovery by Colonel Norris, as noted in his report above referred to, of a block house near the Grand Cañon, of a cache of marten traps near Obsidian Cañon, and other relics of the early trappers.

"In 1863, Captain W. W. De Lacy, in command of a large party of prospectors, left Montana to prospect on the upper waters of the Snake. Striking that river near the junction of Henry's Fork, they followed up the main river through the cañon, prospected in Jackson's Hole; and, not finding gold in paying quantities, they broke up the party, some returning one way, some another. Captain De Lacy, with a portion of the party, followed up the Snake and Lewis Fork, discovering Lewis and Shoshone (De Lacy's) Lakes, the Shoshone and the Lower Geyser Basins. The geographical work done by

Captain De Lacy on this trip was embodied in a map of Montana, drawn by him, and published by authority of the Territory in 1864-65, and the material thus made public was afterward used by the public land office in the compilation of maps of that region.

"The results of this trip seem to have attracted little or no attention; for we hear of no one going into the country until 1869, when two prospectors, Cook and Folsom, made a prospecting tour through the Park. They followed the Yellowstone up to the mouth of the East Fork, then up the latter stream for a few miles, crossing over to the Yellowstone at the Great Falls; thence they went up this stream to the foot of the lake, and around the west side of the latter to the extremity of the west arm, thence crossing over to the Geyser Basins on the Madison, and finally left the country by following down the Madison River. Their story immediately attracted attention, and the following summer a large party, composed of citizens of Montana, under the leadership of General Washburn, then Surveyor-General of Montana, was made up for the purpose of exploring this region. A small escort from Fort Ellis, in charge of Lieut. G. C. Doane, accompanied them.

"This party made quite extensive explorations on the Yellowstone and Madison Rivers. Passing up the Yellowstone by the well-known trail, they traveled completely around the lake, visiting all localities of interest along the route, with the single exception of the Mammoth Hot Springs, on Gardiner's River. While near the head of the lake, Mr. Evarts, a member of the party, became separated from the others, and completely lost. After suffering untold hardships from hunger and cold, rendering him temporarily insane, this gentleman was at last found near the Mammoth Hot Springs.

"The following year, 1871, Captains Barlow and Heep, U. S. A., made a reconnaissance of this country, and presented the results in a brief report and a map of their route.

"In the same year, Dr. Hayden devoted a portion of the season to a reconnaissance of this region, making quite an extended tour through it. The result of this work, including geological reports, maps, etc., were published in the annual report for that year. This was sufficient to fix the public attention upon this great collection of natural wonders, and, when Dr. Hayden presented to Congress a proposition to

HISTORY AND EXPLORATIONS.

reserve this section from settlement as a National Park, it was adopted with little opposition. The following year, 1872, Dr. Hayden continued the reconnaissance of the Park, and the country to the north and south of it, publishing the results in the report of that year, and in a series of maps.

"This region has, ever since its discovery, proved an attractive field for exploration, and scarcely a year has passed that some party, under more or less of official sanction, has not traversed it, nominally, at least, for purposes of exploration.

"In 1873, Captain W. A. Jones, U. S. A., took a large party through it. He entered it from the head of the Stinking Water, crossing one of the many passes near Mount Chittenden (it is impossible to tell which). After visiting most of the points of interest in the Park, he went out *via* the Upper Yellowstone, on the way verifying the old trappers' legend about the 'Two Ocean River,' and discovering a practicable pass (Togwotee Pass) and route from the south to the Park. This discovery was by far the most valuable result of the expedition.

"In 1875, Captain William Ludlow, U. S. A., in charge of a reconnaissance in Central Montana, made a flying trip to the Park. He developed little that was new save accurate measurements of the Upper and Lower Falls of the Yellowstone."

THE UPPER YELLOWSTONE VALLEY.

National Park Branch Railroad. — Livingston is the point on the main line of the Northern Pacific Railroad from which the National Park Branch Line, fifty-one miles in length, is built through the Upper Valley of the Yellowstone, terminating within six miles of the Mammoth Hot Springs.

Livingston is picturesquely situated at the very gate of the Snow Mountains, on the north bank of the river. For 400 miles the flow of the Yellowstone has been eastward, until it mingles with the muddy waters of the Missouri, at Fort Buford, Dakota. At Livingston the course of the stream abruptly changes. To follow it further our faces must be squarely set toward the south, although high mountains seem to bar progress in that direction. Keeping the river on the left hand, after leaving the town, the road passes, for two miles or more, over a gravelly plain, dotted with scattered boulders, and enters the shadow of the terraced and rock-ridged peaks, 3,000 feet in height, through which the stream has carved its way for a distance of three miles, forming its Third or Lower Cañon. This gateway of the mountains leads into a gorge just wide enough to comfortably admit the road alongside the river, the mountain walls rising precipitously on either hand.

Paradise Valley and Prosperous Ranchmen. — Emerging from the Lower Cañon, the road enters at once upon a fertile plain which extends thirty miles up the river, and stretches out to ten or twelve miles in breadth. This is called Paradise Valley. Its fine soil drew settlers to it long ago, when white scalps were much sought after by Indian marauders.

The houses are all built of heavy logs, and are termed "shacks," here as elsewhere throughout the country. Some of them are provided with large, staunch turrets pierced with holes, out of which rifle shots have been often fired in defense of life and home. But fear of Indian attack has now forever passed away.

Owing to the gentle downward slope of the great river, as it traverses this plain, and to the many mountain streams which flow across it, every farm is irrigated at little expense. It is only necessary to dig a shallow ditch, or even plow a long furrow, to conduct sufficient water over the land for raising excellent crops. The settlers praise the climate, speak well of their neighbors, report their wheat yield at forty bushels per acre, their oats abundant and heavy, and their onions, peas, potatoes and other vegetables of wonderful size and prime quality. Indeed, the prosperity of the ranchmen of Paradise Valley is quite evident at a glance. A look of cozy comfort pervades their houses; the door yards are gay with flowers; the barns are full, the hay ricks mighty, the cattle fine and sleek; and the women folk are tidy and cheerful, in harmony with their surroundings. The ranchmen engage largely in stock raising, the rich, plentiful bunch grass of the lower slopes of the mountains affording the best pasturage at all seasons, not excepting winter. One large range in the valley is occupied by a band of two thousand horses, the grade of which is gradually improving, and the annual sale of the increase always insuring a fine income to the owners. In the way of recreation, the farmers shoot elk and antelope, or track a bear in the neighboring hills to its death. The Yellowstone, all through its course in Paradise Valley, is fringed with trees, and has a stony and gravelly bed, with an impetuous current of six or seven miles an hour, a depth of as many feet, and a width of about 100 yards. Its waters, constantly freshened by mountain springs and torrents, are cold and clear, and alive with trout and the equally gamesome grayling. The former range in weight from half a pound to two pounds and upward. They take the fly freely; but the settlers, who only catch them for the pot, lure them with grasshoppers.

Superb Mountain Views.—The Snow Mountains border the river on the south and east, their lofty pinnacles glistening with snow, and presenting views and atmospheric effects which are perfectly superb. Especially striking are those on the east side. A panorama of stately domes is constantly unfolding a succession of the grandest pictures. These mountains lift their well-rounded forms to a height of 3,000 or 4,000 feet above the elevated valley. For a groundwork of color there is the old gold tint of the dried grass that spreads a garment over all the slopes. This is relieved by the "twilight gloom of forests primeval" in the profound ravines that seam and furrow the enormous masses. Sombre gorges, through which foaming torrents plunge down the steeps, harbor in their black recesses the wild creatures of the wood. The bald summits of limestone or granite, having resisted the storms of centuries, stand out in sharp and frowning outline against the cloudless sky, or else veil their awful majesty in fleecy mists or purple haze. But the eye is fascinated, not alone by the glorious mountains to the eastward, there being, as well, many charming accessories of the perfect picture. Yonder is the river, flowing swiftly on past wooded islets which are mirrored on the silver flood; myriads of water fowl flock to the feeding grounds along the shallows; eagles and fish-hawks hover over the plain, while peaceful farmsteads, with groups of cattle in the fields, stud the scene.

On the west side, the mountains are neither so commanding nor impressive. They are, nevertheless, very remarkable, especially from the geological point of view. Born of volcanic forces, their steep and rugged sides show also the mighty power of glacial action. The history of this antique Yellowstone Valley is plainly written upon the rocks. These consist principally of stratified conglomerates and enormous thickness of breccia, the varied coloring of the latter at once attracting attention. At frequent intervals, in ages long ago, streams of lava have coursed down the heights, hardening into basalt or closer textured trachytes. Glaciers have stranded gigantic granite boulders or blocks of gneiss far up the slopes, and deposited other drift materials and moraines upon the levels. The capricious sculpture of wind and water is seen upon the softer material, which has assumed the strangest forms of slender pillars, detached mounds, peaks, pinnacles and other odd and fantastic shapes. One mass of granitoid gneiss, lying far away from the hills, in the middle of the valley, is always taken for a solitary shack. The resemblance is so good that the mistake is unavoidable.

The massive bulk of Emigrant Peak (10,629 feet above the sea, and 6,000 feet above the valley) soon looms up across the river. It is a magnificent height, remarkably fine in outline and rich in color. The sombre gulches of this mountain are full of gold. The washings have already yielded enough of the precious metal for a king's ransom, and the gravel is still paying tribute to a colony of placer miners.

Clark's Fork Mines.—The most important mining district in this part of the country is that of Clark's Fork. Cooke City, the largest camp in the district, is fifty-one miles distant from Livingston, from which town it receives its supplies, and fifty-five miles from Cinnabar, the southern terminus of the Yellowstone Park Branch. Every character of silver-bearing ore is found here, from free-milling quartz to the most refractory galena. The greatest activity prevails, the output in the summer and fall of 1885 reaching 850 tons of ore per day, almost half as much as that of Butte, the most productive mining camp in the world. The ore contains, also, considerable traces of gold, specimens recently assayed having yielded as much as $40 to the ton. The Clark's Fork mines are as yet without railroad communication; but a branch is projected from some convenient point on the Northern Pacific Railroad, and, in view of the growing importance of the mines, its construction can not long be delayed.

The Middle Cañon.—This wild and terrible gorge is nearly three miles in length, and the river, at the narrowest part, is compressed to a width of less than 100 feet. Seen from the crest of the cañon, the savage grandeur of the scene deeply impresses itself upon the beholder. The river rushes tumultuously along the abysmal deep with a deafening roar through the channel which the waters have worn out of the metamorphic rocks of the abutting mountains, whose slopes are dark with timber. Great blocks of gneiss and boulders of granite have fallen from the crags, and lodged at the sides and in the middle of the stream. Around these obstructions, which are mantled with mosses, and upon which a defiant pine is often perched, the green flood lashes into foam, swirling in furious eddies, breaking over half-sunken rocks or tumbling down low cascades, but seldom forming a quiet pool.

The eminent British geologist, Dr. Archibald Geikie, has recently described the physical characteristics of this part of the valley and the Middle Cañon as follows:

"The Yellowstone is a noble stream, winding through a broad alluvial valley, flanked with hills on either side, those on the right, or east bank, towering up into one of the noblest ranges of the Rocky Mountains. Here, as well as on the Madison, we met with illustrations, on a magnificent scale, of the general law of valley structure, that every gorge formed by the convergence of the hills on either side has an expansion of the valley into a lake-like plain on its upper side. For several hours we rode along this plain among mounds of detritus, grouped in that crescent-shaped arrangement so characteristic of glacier moraines. Large blocks of crystalline rock, quite unlike the volcanic masses along which we were traveling, lay tossed about among the mounds.

"There can be no doubt about the massiveness of the

glaciers that once filled up the Valley of the Yellowstone. The moraine mounds extend across the plain, and mount the bases of the hills on either side. The glacier which shed them must, consequently, have been here a mile or more in breadth. All the way up the valley we were on the outlook for evidence as to the thickness of the ice, which might be revealed by the height at which either transported blocks had been stranded, or a polished and striated surface had been left upon the rocks of the valley. We were fortunate in meeting evidence of both kinds.

"I shall not soon forget my astonishment on entering the Second Cañon. We had mounted the hills on the left side, and observed how the detritus (glacial detritus, as we believed it to be) had been re-arranged and spread out into terraces, either by the river, when at a much higher level than that at which it now flows, or by a lake which evidently filled up the broad expansion of the valley between the two lowest cañons. We were prepared, therefore, for the discovery of still more striking proof of the power and magnitude of the old glaciers, but never anticipated that so gigantic and perfect a piece of ice work as the Second Cañon was in store for us. From a narrow gorge, the sides of which rise to heights of 1,000 feet or more, the river darts out into the plain which we had been traversing. The rocky sides of this ravine are smoothly polished and striated from the bottom up apparently to the top. Some of the detached knobs of schist rising out of the plain at the mouth of the cañon were as fresh in their ice polish as if the glacier had only recently retired from them. The scene reminded me more of the valley of the Aar above the Grimsel than of any other European glacier grounds. As we rode up the gorge, with here and there just room to pass between the rushing river and the rocky declivity, we could trace the ice-worn bosses of schist far up the heights till they lost themselves among the pines. The frosts of winter are slowly effacing the surfaces sculptured by the vanished glacier. Huge angular blocks are from time to time detached from the crags, and join the piles of detritus at the bottom. But where the ice-polished surfaces are not much traversed with joints, they have a marvelous power of endurance. Hence they may have utterly disappeared from one part of a rock-face, and remain perfectly preserved on another adjoining part. There can be no doubt now that the Yellowstone glacier was massive enough to fill up the Second Cañon to the brim,—that is to say, it must there have been 800 or 1,000 feet thick. But in the course of our ascent we obtained proof that the thickness was even greater than this; for we found that the ice had perched blocks of granite and gneiss on the sides of the volcanic hills not less than 1,600 feet above the present plane of the river, and that it not merely filled up the main valley, but actually overrode the bounding hills, so as to pass into some of the adjacent valleys. That glaciers once nestled in these mountains might have been readily anticipated; but it was important to be able to demonstrate their former existence, and to show that they attained such a magnitude."

Cinnabar Mountain and the Devil's Slide.—About seven miles from the Middle Cañon, on the right, is Cinnabar Mountain. This is a handsome peak, standing out from the other elevations, and making a fine picture. Its name was probably given because a broad stripe of vermilion hue girdles the height half way up its face; but no trace of cinnabar has been found at this point. The south face of this bare mountain is traversed from apex to base by two enormous dikes of trap-rock, which curve slightly to the right at the summit. These walls are, perhaps, 200 feet high and 50 feet broad, the space between them at the top being about 150 feet, and gradually increasing until it is doubled at the bottom. The material between the dikes has been washed away, leaving the gigantic walls as smooth and vertical as if built by masons' skill. Nature has seldom shown so wonderful a specimen of her handicraft. The broad, level top of each wall is dotted with pine trees, which grow tall and straight, in keeping with their exalted station. The early explorers christened this place "The Devil's Slide," and certainly the perfect plane of bright red and brown clay suggests a slide down hill which no child of earth would willingly attempt. Adjoining this slide are bands of red and yellow, which follow the curve of the dikes, and arrest the eye by their brilliant and contrasting colors.

Cinnabar.—This little town has sprung into existence at the southern terminus of the branch railroad, and within a short distance of the northern boundary of the Park. The six miles remaining to be accomplished before the traveler arrives at the Mammoth Hot Springs, his first stopping place in that enchanted region, are performed by stage, Concord coaches running in connection with all passenger trains.

Gardiner River Valley.—Near Cinnabar, the Yellowstone receives the waters of the Gardiner River, and it is mainly through the valley of the latter stream that the U. S. engineers, charged with the duty of ascertaining the most practicable routes between various points and of building the magnificent roads that have rendered easy of access the innumerable objects of interest in the Park, have constructed the road from the railway terminus to the Mammoth Hot Springs. In this valley, evidences of the volcanic character of the country are more numerous and striking than in that of the Yellowstone. The general scenery, too, is exceedingly grand and imposing, Sepulchre Mountain looming up to the right, in front the fine outline of Bunsen's Peak, and to the east the majestic domes of the Yellowstone Range. Amid such surroundings as these, a sharp turn in the road reveals one of the most curious features of the Park, meeting the traveler at its very threshold.

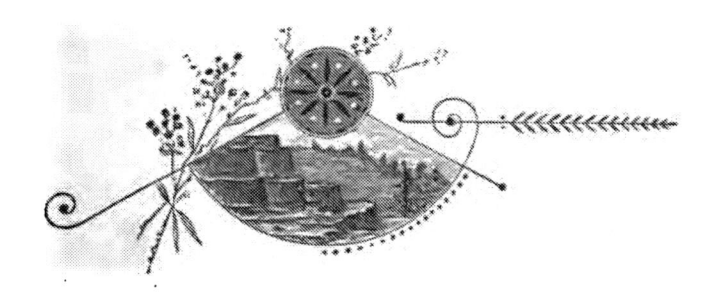

THE MAMMOTH HOT SPRINGS.

These remarkable terrace-building springs are situated in a small valley, 1,000 feet above the Gardiner River, into which their flow is discharged. The material deposited by the springs is mainly calcareous, taken up by the hot water as it finds its way to the surface through deep-lying cretaceous strata. The water issues at various elevations on the terraces from many vents, in pulsating waves, which overflow the basins, and deposit thin, corrugated layers of carbonate of lime as travertine. This deposit is moderately hard while wet, but becomes quite soft and friable as it dries. The slow but ceaseless operation of the springs has resulted in building up terrace after terrace of scallop-edged, limpid pools and basins of hot water of varied size, form and temperature.

A fine view of the most active springs and the surrounding mountains is obtained from an eminence upon which have hitherto stood the headquarters of the Park Superintendent, a building the removal of which is now in contemplation and may be effected at any time. Directly in front looms, through floating clouds of steam, the glaring bulk of the principal snow-white terraces, 200 feet above the plateau at their base. This plateau is pitted with numerous caverns of various depths and sizes, which were once the basins of ancient springs, but are now choked with shrubbery. Groups of pines or single trees find sufficient nutriment in the crumbling calcareous deposit to support themselves.

Liberty Cap and Giant's Thumb.—Toward the northwest corner of this plateau rises an isolated shaft, forty-five feet in height and twenty feet in diameter at the base, the cone

General View of Gardiner River Valley and Hot Springs.

of an extinct geyser. "It is composed," says Dr. A. C. Peale, in his report to Dr. Hayden on the thermal springs of the Yellowstone National Park, under date of August 1st, 1881, "of overlapping layers of sediment, having evidently been built up by the overflow of the water from the orifice at the top. The deposit is hard, of close, compact structure, and of considerable age. Surrounding this cone are a number of shallow basins, some of which are snowy white, tinted with pink. But few active springs are found here at present." One hundred yards or so further west is another cone of the same character, although much inferior in size. These singular objects at once attract attention. The taller cone, from its shape, is aptly named the "Liberty Cap;" the other, which abuts upon the sinter bluff, has been christened the "Giant's Thumb." Both cones show signs of age and decrepitude. Deep fissures yawn in their surfaces, and the weather is gradually crumbling them away. An attempt to restore their original symmetry by conducting streams of water from the hot springs above may succeed. It is hoped that the deposits of lime may gradually fill up the fractures and cavities, and renew the youth of the cones. It would be a pity for these mausoleums of old geysers to crumble into dust.

Climbing the Main Terrace.—The ascent from this point to the main terrace of active springs is not difficult. Stepping upon the first of a series of broad ledges which lead to the base of the terrace, the way is threaded through a maze of rills of hot water, over the low, scalloped rims of limpid, steaming pools, where it seems sacrilege to tread. The novelty and magnificence of the scene are bewildering. Not distance, but proximity, lends enchantment to the view. The brilliancy and variety of the coloring matter about the pools, as well as the delicacy and beauty of the formations, are indescribably wonderful. Terrace after terrace is thus surmounted, some of these eight or ten feet high and several yards in width; others are mere ledges. On each of these levels the water collects in a long tier of nearly semicircular basins, of different diameters, lying close together. The higher terraces present an imposing front, the contour of their scalloped margins at once suggesting frozen water-falls. Over the rims of the basins on the topmost level the water gently pours until it finds its way into the reservoirs next below, repeating this process till the bottom of the hill is reached, where the flow is collected, and carried off by several channels to the Gardiner River.

Exquisite Formations and Splendid Colors.—The deposits which result from evaporation at the margin of each basin are exquisite in form and color. The rims are fretted with a delicate frost-work, and the outside of each bowl is beautifully adorned with a honeycomb pattern, while the spaces between the curves are often filled with glistening stalactites. The coating of the sides of the basins and pools takes on every delicate and vivid tint, rich cream and salmon colors predominating, but these deepening near the edges into brilliant shades of red, brown, green and yellow. The largest springs, supplying most of the water to the tiers of bowls on each of the terraces, are situated on a broad, level space covering some acres at the top of the hill. One has a basin forty feet in length by twenty-five in width. Others are nearly as great. The water is a turquoise blue, and so perfectly translucent that the most microscopic fretting deep down upon the sides and bottoms of the pools is plainly visible. This is the case with the hot-spring water everywhere. Its crystal clearness can not be described; it must be seen to be appreciated. The crust between the springs seems rather treacherous to the foot, and it is impossible to get about without soaking the shoes in hot water. Most of the springs have two centres of ebullition, at which, doubtless, the water is at the boiling point; but at the edges the temperature is much lower. Around the hottest pools, in many cases, there are strung along the rim, like beads

General View of Mammoth Hot Springs and Pulpit Terraces.

on a necklace, a row of nodules as large as hazel nuts and hard as adamant. The play of the waters as they seethe up from the cavernous throats of the pools and undulate in miniature waves is wonderful. The rays of light are refracted by the agitation upon the surface, and are resolved into all the colors of the prism.

In several places beneath the crust the rush and gurgle of flowing water is distinctly heard. There is one cleft, a foot or more in width, revealing a steaming stream traceable over a hundred yards in its course to the flashing pools below. The hot-water vegetation is a curious feature of all the cooler rills which flow from the boiling springs. There is an abundance of yellow, green, red, white and brown confervæ, covered with sulphur, which stream in long threads of silken texture through the gullies. These streaming filaments are very pretty.

Cleopatra Spring.—Among the principal springs is the Cleopatra, so named by some of the earlier visitors. It is the most beautiful in the basin. It is situated on a mound of deposit which is forty feet in height, and covers an area of three-quarters of an acre. Dr. Peale describes it as follows: " The spring has light blue tinted water in a white basin, with light yellowish red edges. A large flat basin surrounds the spring. At the east end are basins lined with reddish tufted material. The greatest overflow escapes at the west end, and the basins here are fringed with stalactitic masses. The basin at the edge of which these stalactites are most prominent is eight feet high. Below it the water flows over an incline, at the base of which are handsome white, red and yellow basins. The whole front of the mass is lined with these basins, and on the west side, where the overflow was in 1871, they are snowy white. The amount of water is very small in comparison with the amount of deposit. It sinks out of sight at the base of the mass. This spring has a temperature of 154° at the edge. As the water escapes, it flows over a ladder that has been placed against the edge, for the purpose of coating articles that are hung on it. The rate of deposition, under favorable circumstances, is about one-sixteenth of an inch in four days (96 hours). It is almost impossible to describe this mass and the basins that compose it, in words. The spring is 20 feet below the terrace immediately back of it."

Extinct Spring Terraces.—The distance from the principal group of active hot springs to the nearest point on Gardiner River is about one mile. A hard scramble over the rough declivities of several intervening extinct spring terraces and through an occasional belt of timber is the penalty of making it. Numerous deep pits, now overgrown with bushes and scrubby pines, show the places which once were pools. Below the pits the scalloped rims of former basins are distinctly seen, and well-rounded geyser cones are also sometimes noticed. Doubtless in earlier times the chief centre of boiling-spring activity was about midway between the river and its present scene. Many of the pines which have grown out of the ancient deposit are large and stately, perhaps 80 or 100 years of age. Their flourishing condition is in strong contrast with that of the trees in the neighborhood of the active springs. The deposit of travertine has doomed to destruction all the forest growth that lies in its course. It has already banked itself around hundreds of trees on the slope of the hill where the hot springs are now at work, covering them to the depth of several feet, and its encroachments steadily continue. Numbers of these blasted, helpless pines still stand erect, looking quite dismal imbedded in snow-white travertine which almost touches their leafless branches.

This calcareous deposit covers an area of three square miles. Of this, the recent deposits, on which the springs are at present found, occupy about 170 acres. Along the river bank there are still many active boiling springs. For a mile up the hillside there is terrace after terrace of extinct springs. Then comes the principal point of present activity, which extends with gradually waning power over a distance of a mile into the dense woods on the top of the mountain. There are fourteen well-defined terraces within the bounds mentioned, which are now, or have been at one time, the scene of boiling-spring activity.

Although the Mammoth Hot Springs are by far the most important of the kind now active in the world, they are insignificant as compared with what they were when they built Terrace Mountain; or to what other springs were, perhaps, at the same period, which resulted in the formation of the immense cliffs along the Yellowstone at Bear Gulch, at Sheep-eater Cliff, and many other localities where these enormous deposits, now destitute of active springs, are slowly crumbling away.

Dr. Geikie thus describes these springs:

"The first glimpse of this singular scene, caught from a crest of the dividing ridge, recalls the termination of a glacier. A mass of snowy whiteness protrudes from a lateral pine valley, and presents a steep front to the narrow plain at its base. The contrast between it and the sombre hue of the pines all round, heightens the resemblance of its form and aspect to a mass of ice. It is all rock, however, deposited by the hot water which, issuing from innumerable openings down the valley, has in course of time filled it up with white sinter. Columns of steam rising from the mass, bear witness even at a distance to the nature of the locality. We wandered over this singular accumulation, each of us searching for a pool of water cool enough to be used as a bath. I found one where the water, after quitting its conduit, made a circuit round a basin of sinter, and in so doing cooled down sufficiently to let one sit in it. The top of the mound, and, indeed, those parts of the deposits generally, from which the water has retreated, and which are therefore dried and exposed to the weather, are apt to crack into thin shells, or to crumble into white powder. But along the steep front from which most of the springs escape, the water collects into basins at many different levels. Each of these basins has the most exquisitely fretted rim. It is at their margin that evaporation proceeds most vigorously and deposition takes place most rapidly; hence the rim is being constantly added to. The colors of these wavy, frill-like borders are sometimes remarkably vivid. The contrast between the heat below and the cold above ground at nights, is sometimes very great. We used to rise about daybreak, and, repairing to the nearest brook or river for ablution, sometimes found a crust of ice on its quiet pools."

Medicinal.—The healing qualities of the Gardiner River hot springs have never been fully tested. A complete analysis of the waters has yet to be made. Persons afflicted with rheumatism and eruptive diseases have found relief by bathing in the hot springs near the bank of the Gardiner River. The water is rather agreeable to the taste, and remarkably soft to the touch. It is very pleasant to the skin, and has an invigorating effect on the body. Should investigation prove that these springs possess extraordinary medicinal virtues, it is likely that the place will early become a resort for the afflicted, as well as for the admirers of novel and beautiful scenes. The high and noble mountains which entirely surround the Mammoth Hot Springs give a charming landscape picture to the situation.

Trout Fishing Extraordinary.—It has often been said that it is possible to catch trout in the Yellowstone Lake and cook them in a boiling spring close behind the angler, without taking them off the hook. This assertion seems incredible, and it is generally doubted. But this extraordinary feat may certainly be accomplished, not only at the Yellowstone Lake, but also on the Gardiner River, below the Mammoth Hot Springs. The writer performed it at the latter place, in the presence of nine witnesses, at a point not far from a deserted cabin at the foot of the long series of terraces. Selecting a likely pool of the ice-cold stream, with a boiling spring fifteen feet distant from the bank, he stood upon a projecting rock and made a cast. His fly soon tempted a trout to his doom. The fish was small enough to be lifted out of the water without the aid of a landing net, and it was quite easy to drop him into the bubbling hot spring behind. His life must have been extinguished instantly. This procedure was repeated several times, and each of the spectators who had purposely assembled to test the truth of the strange assertion, partook of the fish thus caught and boiled. It required from three to five minutes to thoroughly cook the victims of the experiment, and it was the general verdict that they only needed a little salt to make them quite palatable. This is a "fish story," without doubt, but a perfectly true one. A feat so extraordinary could nowhere else be practiced. It must be chronicled as one of the marvels of the National Park. There are several other places in this land of wonders besides those named where this fishing extraordinary could be successfully attempted.

Middle Falls of the Gardiner River.—The cañon and Middle Falls, about four miles due south from the Mammoth Hot Springs, are reached by a rough trail. The cañon is about forty yards wide at its base, and 500 yards across at its top. Its depth is from 1,200 to 1,500 feet. The falls are of singular grace and beauty. The river seems to rise above the clouds, and rushes down a descent of 300 feet, one-third of which is an unbroken fall. The steep and rugged sides of the cañon, as well as its margin, are densely wooded with a growth of scrub pine. Above the falls the cliffs are like battlements, with here and there a tall spire. At a little distance, so symmetrical are the different outflows of basalt, the columnar formations appear to be the work of art. The cañon is many miles in length, and is scarcely inferior to that of the Yellowstone in wild grandeur. The path, after winding picturesquely along the sides of Bunsen's Peak, leads out into a rolling prairie, interspersed with reed-fringed ponds. From the summit of any hillock there is seen in every direction the dark forest, which spreads out in terraces to the horizon, its green

86   YELLOWSTONE NATIONAL PARK.

mantle perforated in the distance by the protruding peaks of the Shoshone and Madison ranges, while still further southward the three Tetons tower upward like watch-towers. Sheep-eater Cliffs, which lie eastward, are passed, and three miles from the falls the main road to the Geyser Basins is reached near Swan Lake.

Grand Tour of the Park.

The chief attractions of the grand tour comprise the Golden Gate, the Obsidian Cliffs, the Norris Geyser Basin, Virginia Cañon and Cascades, the Grand Cañon, and Upper and Lower Falls of the Yellowstone River, the view from Mt. Washburn, Tower Falls, thence southward to Yellowstone Lake and Mud Geysers, Crater Hill, and Mary's Mountain road to Firehole or Middle Geyser Basin, the Excelsior and Upper Geyser Basin; and returning, Gibbon Falls, Gibbon Paint Pots, and Mt. Schurz, between the Middle and the Norris Geyser Basins. These places of interest are, with three unimportant exceptions, embraced within the round trip of the stages, which run daily from about June 15 to October 1. The roads, which have been admirably constructed, and are kept in remarkably good condition, considering the small amount annually appropriated by Congress for the maintenance of the Park, have been laid out with a view to rendering it practicable to visit all the points of especial interest without traversing the same road twice. While this desirable end has not yet been fully attained, its accomplishment is proceeding rapidly.

During the summer of 1889, for example, will be commenced a road from the Great Falls by way of the Cañon and Tower Falls to Yancey's, on the Cook City road. This will save many miles of doubling, and allow a longer time than heretofore at places of transcendent interest. The starting-point for the grand tour is Mammoth Hot Springs. While stop-over privileges are granted at all points where hotel accommodations are provided, and opportunity is afforded for special excursions to such objects of interest as can not conveniently be embraced within the regular tour, there is nothing to be gained, but, on the contrary, much to be

Lake of the Woods and Obsidian Cliffs.

lost, by any material deviation from the route laid down in these pages. That route has many advantages, not the least of them consisting in the fact that the wonders of the Park are visited in such sequence that the interest, astonishment and delight of the traveler increase with each succeeding stage of the tour, until the crowning glory of the entire region is reached in the Grand Cañon of the Yellowstone.

Golden Gate and Kingman's Pass.—After leaving Mammoth Hot Springs, the road, which formerly crossed Terrace Mountain, and was as difficult as it was circuitous, proceeds almost directly southward through a magnificent defile, where the skill employed in its construction, and the substantial character of the work, claim constant admiration. One of the minor objects of interest in this land of wonders is the Rustic Falls, on Glenn Creek, one of the tributaries of the Gardiner River, to the left of the road. The stream is fed by the mountain snows, and takes its course for a mile or so through a sage-brush plain. It then falls fifty or sixty feet into a series of shallow basins, which it has worn out of the moss-covered rock. The fall is very gentle, and the flowers and waving ferns, which cling to the sides of the chasm, are kept fresh and bright by the spray, which lightly touches them. The cañon below the falls rapidly widens and deepens into a gloomy, impassable gorge. In the open valley above, and upon a timbered ledge overhanging the falls, are vestiges of a Sheep-eater Indian camp and a driveway for game. Four miles from Mammoth Hot Springs, the road reaches a pretty little sheet of water, named Swan Lake. The fallen timber on the hill-sides, laid by the wind, forms perfect *chevaux-de-frise*. Two and a half miles beyond, the Middle Fork of the Gardiner River is reached, the valley of which stream is followed to the upper end of Willow Park.

The Obsidian or Volcanic Glass Cliffs.—The Obsidian Cliffs are a mile and a half south of Willow Park. These cliffs rise like basalt in almost vertical columns from the eastern shores of Beaver Lake, and are probably unequaled in the world. They are from 150 to 250 feet in height, and 1,000 feet in length, although there are croppings of the same material to be traced as far as the Lake of the Woods, two miles beyond. This volcanic glass glistens like jet, but is quite opaque. Sometimes it is variegated with streaks of red and yellow. Large blocks of it have been, from time to time, detached, forming a sloping barricade at an angle of 45° to the hot springs at the margin of Beaver Lake. It was necessary to build a carriage road over these blocks. This was accomplished by Colonel Norris, late Superintendent of the Park, by building great fires upon the largest masses, which, after they had been sufficiently expanded by the heat, were suddenly cooled by dashing cold water over them. This had the effect of fracturing the blocks into fragments which could be handled, and a glass carriage-way, a quarter of a mile in length, was made. Without doubt, this is the only piece of glass road in the world. Blocks of obsidian are to be found along the Gardiner River for a few miles below the cliffs, and the whole region from Paradise Valley, in the Upper Yellowstone, southward, is strewn with chips and pebbles of this material. On the bays of the Yellowstone Lake, and in many of the clear stream beds, tiny fragments of obsidian are to be seen glittering like gems.

Obsidian is a species of lava, which, according to Pliny, was first found in Ethiopia. The name, however, seems to have been applied by the ancients to Chian marble, and is probably a false spelling of the Greek *opsianus*, signifying to reflect images, because the Chian marble was as hard to cut as the volcanic glass, and was used for mirrors.

The Indians used this glass in making arrow-heads, weapons and tools. Relics of this sort, which tourists find, seem to be made of the superior quality of obsidian which was procured at the cliffs. An impure variety, black with white flecks, is common at other points within the Park, notably near the Great Falls of the Yellowstone, at Crystal Cascades, and near Shoshone Lake on the Continental Divide.

Beaver Lake.—This is a beautiful sheet of water, half a mile in width and more than a mile in length. It is of considerable depth, and is the haunt of numbers of wild geese, ducks, cranes and other water fowl. Its swampy margin is covered with lily-pads, and along its borders are to be found many fine specimens of the flora of the Park. Around its wooded, hilly shores, there are numerous hot and cold springs, and at the southern end of the lake is a large flat where Green Creek pours into it. This lake was formed by beavers, which have obstructed the creek and constructed a series of three or four dams, which sweep in graceful curves from side to side, each having a fall of from two to three feet in a distance of two miles. The road flanks the lake for nearly a mile, and then takes a westward sweep, crossing, by a comparatively easy pass, the divide which separates the waters of Gardiner River, flowing into the Yellowstone, from those of the Gibbon, which are tributary to the Madison River. This ridge surmounted, the first active geysers come suddenly into view.

Norris Geyser Basin.—This Basin is doubtless the oldest and highest in the Park, revealing much that is wonderful and attractive. It is apt to astonish and bewilder the neophyte in Wonderland, by its spouting geysers, clouds of vapor and overpowering odors of sulphur, it being the first "fire-hole" area encountered on entering the Park. The whole vast Basin is a collection of hot springs and pools varying greatly in color, some being jet black, some white as driven snow on mountain height, and others as sulphurous a yellow as Lucifer could desire. There are numerous fumaroles and solfatari, besides "frying-pans" which sputter and sizzle violently. The earth rumbles and shakes, and the air is hot, and reeks with unpleasant odors. Where the water does not boil over the

Norris Geyser Basin—Monarch Geyser in Action.

crust, it seethes and gurgles beneath, rendering great caution necessary in getting about on the treacherous surface. Numbers of the steam vents are adorned with beautiful sulphur crystals, and masses of this material are heaped in every direction. Some of the springs are "paint pots," which boil incessantly their pasty clay of divers colors, with noisy sputtering. Among the geysers in the plateau toward the southwest are the "Constant," the "Twins" and the "Triplets," which seem to be in perpetual action, obscuring the sun's rays with their steam ; and on the highest point of the ridge, a few paces to the right of the road, is a large mud pot, which discharges at frequent intervals a heavy jet of pale-drab spray, eight to ten feet high, which spreads out like a bush of coral. A smoke hole near by, on the verge of the road, sends out, with rumble and awful roar, blasts of superheated steam. This is named "Steamboat Vent." There are two roaring steam holes which, says Dr. Peale, "look as though they had just burst through the surface, and the gully leading toward the ravine to the south is covered with sand that appears to have been poured out during an eruption. Trees standing in the line of this sand-flood are dead, and a number are uprooted, and covered with sand. Everything seems to point to the fact of the recent formation of this vent. There is no deposit marking the opening, although stones surrounding the hole are beginning to have points of geyserite deposited on their upper surfaces." Colonel Norris says that this vent had no existence in 1875, but that in 1878 it had become a powerful flowing geyser. This promises to be one of the most interesting geysers in the Park, as it will afford most important data as to the building of the deposits and the age of the geysers. On the left of the road, within a rod or two of the mud pot, is the "Emerald Pool," its large, deep bowl brim full of purest water of the bluish green tint of a beryl.

Southeastward a few yards the Fissure, or New Crater Geyser, throws a shower of glistening drops at short intervals.

To the left, on the road at the foot of the ridge, is the "Minute Man," who faithfully spurts, once in sixty seconds, a bold stream to the height of twenty-five or thirty feet, from an orifice in the rock about six inches in diameter. To the east, near the bluff, in a small cove, enthroned among rough boulders of gorgeous colors, is the "Monarch." He spouts in regal splendor, once in twenty-four hours, a stream from 100 to 125 feet high, through three elongated orifices, respectively 2 by 12, $2\frac{1}{2}$ by 11, and 5 by 6 feet in dimensions. The eruption continues about twenty minutes, and the flow of hot water is immense. The "Fearless" is next seen, its funnel-shaped crater spouting dark-green water, which shades off at the margin of the Basin into pale-green and violet tints.

From Norris Geyser Basin to the Great Falls.— During the summer of 1886 and 1887 the Virginia Cañon road was opened to travel. This enables the tourists to make the journey from the Mammoth Hot Springs to the Grand Cañon between the hours of 8 A. M. and 3 P. M., reaching the Norris Hotel for dinner, and avoiding the tedious ride, before necessary, from Lower Geyser Basin over Mary's Mountain, a distance of thirty miles, which had to be retraced upon the return trip.

VIRGINIA CANON ROAD TO THE FALLS.

Following the Virginia Cañon road some three miles from the Norris Geyser Basin, we enter one of the most charming and picturesque of cañons upon the entire trip. It can not be compared in point of size and color with its near neighbor of the Yellowstone; but it gives a certain satisfaction, hard to be accounted for. The road leads up the Cañon at a gentle grade. The Cañon narrows and becomes more rugged. High pinnacles of weather-scarred rock tower above us. Fantastic shapes and heavy shadows confront us at every turn, fitly preparing one for the delightful view of Virginia Cascades. The crystal water rushing and hurrying down over the comparatively smooth incline of dark moss-covered rock. So finely is it broken and so rapid is its descent that at first glance it seems to wrought-up imagination, like a huge sheet of frosted and fretted silver, stretched downward from the Cañon head. The fall is about seventy-five feet; but framed as it is by the sombre rock and darker pine, its fitness and completeness is equaled by few of all the sights in this land of wonders.

Climbing a steep grade out of the Cañon, and following up the stream a short distance, we gradually ascend and cross the continental divide. Glimpses of the Yellowstone Valley are occasionally caught as the tourist follows the rapidly descending road. At an elevation of some 7,700 feet, and near the river, the old road is joined. A short distance further through the woods, occasionally within sight of the river, after a drive of about eleven and one-half miles, the tourist reaches the hotel at the falls.

During the summer of 1889 the hotel accommodations will be much improved by the erection of a new and commodious hotel at this point.

Upper Falls of the Yellowstone.

THE YELLOWSTONE RIVER AND UPPER FALLS.

The Yellowstone River.—Between the Lake and Upper Fall the river flows for several miles with a strong and steady current through a broad valley, the shores of which are low and grass-clad. The surface of the bright green water is unbroken by rock or rapid, until within about a mile of the place where the river gathers itself together to charge against the phalanx of mountains which oppose its passage northward. The contraction of the valley is quite abrupt, and the river suddenly heaps itself up in its narrow channel, flowing with wild tumult and resistless power, forcing its way over rocks and ledges, and a series of beautiful cascades, until it takes its first mad plunge into the Grand Cañon, which it has carved for over twenty miles through the flanks of the range.

A few hundred yards above the first cataract, three isolated and water-worn rocks tower high above the surge. They are set across the torrent like the piers of an ancient bridge, offering a feeble protest against the progress of the river to its leap of 112 feet at the Upper Fall. These picturesque rocks are partially mantled with stunted and moss-grown shrubs, and upon the tallest towers a thrifty pine.

The Upper Fall.—Long before the Upper Fall reveals itself to the expectant eye, the sullen roar of the water, as it descends into the gorge, is distinctly heard. The cliffs which confine this stream are 200 to 300 feet in height, and the distance from bank to bank, at the edge of the fall, is about eighty feet. Tossing and tearing, fretting and fuming, between these caverned and brightly mottled cliffs, the water churns itself into creamy foam. Reaching the fall, the torrent shoots out into the air far beyond the brink, and drops, in almost unbroken volume, and with great concussion, upon a partially submerged reef, into the deep-lying horseshoe basin, 112 feet below. Rebounding from the rocks, it darts forward in fan-shaped surges, which spread over the sea-green surface of the pool, and sends up, at the same time, dense clouds of spray and mist, which fully veil the lower third of the cataract, and lodge upon the moss-covered walls of the basin, to return again in countless rills to the stream. The Upper Fall is not so large or so grand as the lower; but, perhaps, from the purely artistic point of view, it is more attractive. It is full of life and action, possessing a beauty peculiar to itself. Set in the midst of savagely romantic scenery, and almost secluded from view by the sombre pine forest, it presents a picture which the most celebrated of landscape painters would shrink from attempting to put on canvas. What it lacks in size and power is fully made up by the great display of color, and the singular forms of stratification which distinguish its surroundings. A trail leads down to the brink of the cataract, and jutting lava rocks below afford fine opportunities for observation. The height of the Upper Fall has usually been exaggerated, Capt. Jones, U. S. A., in 1873, finding it by barometric measurement to be 150.2. Upon this point, Mr. Gannett, of the U. S. Geological Survey of 1878, reports authoritatively as follows:

"This year I was enabled to make careful direct measurements by means of cords, and have obtained results which may be depended upon. The Upper Fall was measured by dropping a weighted line from the top of the overhanging cliff, immediately adjoining the fall, to the level of the water at its base, thus obtaining as correct a measurement as could be desired. This measurement gave 112 feet as the clear height of the fall. This result, as compared with the height (140 feet) which I obtained in 1872, from barometric measurement, simply gives another illustration of the uncertainty attending such work, even when made under the most favorable circumstances. In this, and in other similar cases, the fact that the height, as measured by barometer, is greater than the true height, it seems to me, may be explained by the downward rush of air at the lower station, which, of course, would produce an abnormal pressure at that point."

The Falls of Cascade Creek.—Between the Upper and Lower Falls the distance is only half a mile, and, midway of this interval, on the western side, are the Crystal Cascades, three in number, giving a total fall of 129 feet, on Cascade Creek, a small stream which heads in the southern slopes of the Washburn Range. The Creek is crossed by a stout bridge about forty feet above the wonderfully beautiful Grotto Pool, lying between the Upper and Lower Cascades, which are respectively twenty-one and fifty feet in height. Substantial ladders conduct to a grotto. The Falls of Cascade Creek are picturesque in the extreme; but their attractions are overwhelmed by the grandeur to which they are in propinquity. They are simply accessories of the marvelous surroundings. The only opportunity for fishing, in the neighborhood of the Falls, is by descending Cascade Creek to the Yellowstone. The fish are plentiful, and in good condition.

The Great Fall.—Releasing itself from the deep, symmetrical pool at the foot of the Upper Fall, the river turns somewhat abruptly to the left, making its impetuous way through the high bluffs of a wild, pine-clad gorge over low ledges and fragments of rock, until its sea-green water leaps from the brink of the Great Fall into the profound, abysmal solitude of the Grand Cañon, about 350 feet deeper. Think of this amazing plunge! The edge of the Great Fall is not so regular in outline as that of the Upper. Its contour was formerly smooth; but the water is wearing great notches in the rock. One such rock on the jagged verge bears a close resemblance to a colossal human head. The face, as seen from the left bank of the fall, is in profile, the eye sunken under a matted growth of locks, the nose sharply defined, and the lip covered with a long,

Great Falls of the Yellowstone River.

drooping mustache, with which the water plays. The scene from the brink of the fall, looking into the profound depth of the cañon, is of strange majesty and is indescribably awe-inspiring. A roomy platform at the edge of the fall, with a stanch railing on the river side, affords a very good view of the river preparing for its leap. The advancing volume of water flows rapidly but solidly to the brink, and falls with a tremendous shock into a large, circular, foaming caldron, bounded by steep cliffs 800 feet high. The masses of water seem to break into fleecy columns and sheets of glistening foam as they descend; but they nevertheless strike the surface of the pool below with a concussion so heavy that they are forced upward in fountains of spray and clouds of mist which wash the sides of the cañon, nourishing a rank growth of mosses and algæ of every shade of green, ochre, orange, saffron, red, scarlet and brown.

Recovering from the shock of the plunge, the river finds its outlet through a narrow throat at the foot of the pool, appearing in the distance like a streaming ribbon of satin laid along the depths of the Grand Cañon, behind the winding walls of which it is lost to view.

With respect to the height of the Great Fall, the authority of Mr. Gannett is also quoted. He says:

"My measurement of the Lower Fall was not as simple in method, and allows more room for error, than in the case of the Upper Fall. I found a point, by means of the clinometer, on the eastern wall of the cañon, and very near the fall, at the same level as its top. Thence I stretched the line down the cañon wall to the level of the foot of the fall, reaching it at a point so close that we received a thorough drenching from the spray. Then, with the clinometer, I measured, as accurately as possible, the angle of inclination of the line. This gave as the height 297 feet. Though this result can not be regarded as strictly accurate, still its error must be small, and, in round numbers, 300 feet may be regarded as a close approximation to the true height. Ludlow measured this fall directly by means of a sounding line, obtaining 310 feet as the height, a result agreeing quite closely with mine, especially when one reflects on the difficulty of determining when the weight was at the base of the fall, in the cloud of mist and the rushing river. Most of the other measurements are barometric. Such was that of Captain Jones, who gave a height of 328.7 feet."

Both the Upper and Lower Falls are alike in terrible majesty and power; but each, nevertheless, has its peculiar characteristics. The first is partly veiled by the woods, while the other, imprisoned by rugged walls of basalt, dashes itself in mad frenzy into the depths, where the course of the river is actually hidden for a time by the dense clouds of mist and columns of spray which dart upward from the base of the tremendous cataract. If the sun's rays penetrate these mist clouds at the proper angle, there is at once visible a rainbow not only wider but richer in color than can anywhere else be seen.

A bridle path leads to an eminence one mile below the Great Fall, called Lookout Point. From this bluff the most satisfactory view of the raging torrent and of both faces of the cañon is to be obtained.

The Grand Cañon.—This wonderful gorge displays itself from Lookout Point as a scene of enchantment, surpassing every expectation which the imagination has conjured up ere its remarkable features are witnessed. From the Upper Falls, for a distance of eight miles down the stream, the Grand Cañon of the Yellowstone reveals the most varied and astonishing groupings of crags and rocks which eye ever beheld. Among them are many hot springs, one of which is particularly noticeable as it shoots up clouds of vapor from its vent at the apex of a tall pinnacle. Not alone is the gaze entranced by the great variety in the form of the towering rocks which open up in changing pictures like the shifting scenes of a theatre, but also by the marvelous magnificence of this gorge throughout its vast depth in the brilliant tints of every hue, which the hot springs through long eras have painted upon its steeps. Some of the colors are as bright as those to be found

View in the Grand Cañon.

in a box of paints; indeed, it would be difficult to exaggerate their brilliancy. These colors often blend in harmonious shades, especially in the case of reds and yellows, which are toned down by gradual stages to white of purest beauty. Riding along the brink of the cañon, a succession of views present themselves which are awe-inspiring in their grandeur and sublimity. At our feet, far below us, rise pinnacles and towers, so lofty as to mock the masonry of man. In some places the walls of the cañon are vertical; in others they slope gently from the top, appearing like Gothic arches, with their apexes on the brow, and flaring down to the water's edge. The ravines between these arches are filled with growths of pine, which serve as a background for the masses of color on the intervening rocks, bringing out the varied tints in bold relief. Here and there are grand walls of structural basalt, each successive layer showing the jointing so distinctly as to appear like the work of Titanic builders. The nests of eagles and fish-hawks are seen on the pinnacles of the rocks far below, and the view of these birds soaring between the cañon walls, and darting into the stream for trout, is in itself very curious. In addition to all this, there is the silver glimmer of the clear, swift-flowing waters in the depths of the cañon, the whole uniting to form a scene of enchanting splendor. Such views repeat themselves in infinite variety.

Of all the descriptions of the Grand Cañon which have been written, that of the Rev. Dr. Wayland Hoyt may be considered among the most graphic and beautiful. He says:

"Well, we have reached Cascade Creek at last; and a beautiful grove of trees, beneath whose shade sparkles a clear stream, whose waters are free from the nauseous taste of alkali, furnishes a delightful place in which to camp. Now—dismounting, and seeing that your horse is well cared for, while the men are unloading the pack-mules and pitching the tents—walk up that trail winding up that hillside; follow it for a little among the solemn pines, and then pass out from the tree shadows, and take your stand upon that jutting rock,—clinging to it well meanwhile, and being very sure of your footing, for your head will surely grow dizzy,—and there opens before you one of the most stupendous scenes of Nature,—THE LOWER FALLS AND THE AWFUL CAÑON OF THE YELLOWSTONE.

"And now, where shall I begin? and how shall I, in any wise, describe this tremendous sight,—its overpowering grandeur, and, at the same time, its inexpressible beauty?

"Look yonder—those are the Lower Falls of the Yellowstone. They are not the grandest in the world; but there are none more beautiful. There is not the breadth and dash of Niagara, nor is there the enormous depth of leap of some of the waterfalls of the Yosemite. But here is majesty of its own kind, and beauty too. On either side are vast pinnacles of sculptured rock. There, where the rock opens for the river, its waters are compressed from a width of 200 feet between the Upper and Lower Falls to 100 feet where it takes the plunge. The shelf of rock over which it leaps is absolutely level. The water seems to wait a moment on its verge; then it passes with a single bound of 300 feet into the gorge below. It is a sheer, unbroken, compact, shining mass of silver foam. But your eyes are all the time distracted from the fall itself, great and beautiful as it is, to its marvelous setting,—to the surprising, overmastering cañon into which the river leaps, and through which it flows, dwindling to but a foamy ribbon there in its appalling depths. As you cling here to this jutting rock the falls are already many hundred feet below you. The falls unroll their whiteness down amid the cañon glooms. * * * These rocky sides are almost perpendicular; indeed, in many places the boiling springs have gouged them out so as to leave overhanging cliffs and tables at the top. Take a stone and throw it over,—you must wait long before you hear it strike. Nothing more awful have I ever seen than the yawning of that chasm. And the stillness, solemn as midnight, profound as death! The water dashing there, as in a kind of agony, against those rocks, you can not hear. The mighty distance lays the finger of silence on its white lips. You are oppressed with a sense of danger. It is as though the vastness would soon force you from the rock to which you cling. The silence, the sheer depth, the gloom, burden you. It is a relief to feel the firm earth beneath your feet again, as you carefully crawl back from your perching place.

"But this is not all, nor is the half yet told. As soon as you can stand it, go out on that jutting rock again and mark the sculpturing of God upon those vast and solemn walls. By dash of wind and wave, by forces of the frost, by file of snow plunge and glacier and mountain torrent, by the hot breath of boiling springs, those walls have been cut into the most various and surprising shapes. I have seen the middle age castles along the Rhine: there those castles are reproduced exactly. I have seen the soaring summits of the great cathedral spires in the country beyond the sea: there they stand in prototype, only loftier and sublimer.

"And then, of course, and almost beyond all else, you are fascinated by the magnificence and utter opulence of color. Those are not simply gray and hoary depths and reaches and domes and pinnacles of sullen rock. The whole gorge flames. It is as though rainbows had fallen out of the sky and hung themselves there like glorious banners. The underlying color is the clearest yellow; this flushes onward into orange. Down at the base the deepest mosses unroll their draperies of the most vivid green; browns, sweet and soft, do their blending; white rocks stand spectral; turrets of rock shoot up as crimson as though they were drenched through with blood. It is a wilderness of color. It is impossible that even the pencil of an artist can tell it. What you would call, accustomed to the softer tints of nature, a great exaggeration, would be the utmost tameness compared with the reality. It is as though the most glorious sunset you ever saw had been caught and held upon that resplendent, awful gorge.

"Through nearly all the hours of that afternoon until the sunset shadows came, and afterward, amid the moonbeams, I waited there, clinging to that rock, jutting out into that overpowering, gorgeous chasm. I was appalled and fascinated, afraid and yet compelled to cling there. It was an epoch in my life."

The Painted Cliffs.—About four miles below the Great Falls, at the eastern end of an open meadow, is a trail which diverges from the new bridle-path to Tower Falls, and leads two miles beyond to a part of the cañon which is well worth visiting. The object of attraction is the beautiful coloring of the cliffs in this locality, the result of hot spring deposits. "The yellows," says Dr. Peale, "which are so brilliant and widespread, are due to sulphur, and the reds to the oxidation of iron." Looking up the river to the left, the walls of the cañon have been undermined by the springs, and slipped across the bed of the stream. The enormous slopes of talus are mainly covered with pines; but there are many great patches of brown and white. To the right, and upon a high hill in the foreground, the coloring is in strong and brilliant contrast to that on the left. The broad, precipitous slope from the brow of the cañon to the river appears like a gorgeous flag spread out with stripes of red, white and yellow. From the foot of a tall tower, half way up the slope, broad streamers of red and white open out like a fan and trail down to the silver river, sifting in dazzling brightness through the trees. The red is of the deepest tint, blending into shades of scarlet and orange. So wonderful a display of color is only to be looked for in the sunset heavens. Giant cliffs hem in the river at the foot of the steep slopes, the rugged and eroded faces of which are "grand, gloomy and peculiar." The view altogether is weird and appalling, while the profound solitude and absolute silence impress the beholder with an overwhelming sense of his own insignificance.

On the depth of the Grand Cañon Mr. Gannett's report is again quoted as that of the most trustworthy investigator. He says:

"Commencing at the falls, the Grand Cañon extends down nearly to the mouth of the East Fork, a distance, as the river flows, of twenty-four miles. Indeed, from the falls to the mouth of Gardiner's River, the Yellowstone is in a continuous cañon; but the partial break at the mouth of the East Fork separates it into two parts, known as the Grand and the Third Cañons. The former occupies the line of greatest depression in a volcanic plateau, which slopes to the northward and southward from the Washburn group of mountains, and to the westward from the Amethyst Ridge of the Yellowstone Range. Its course is northeast as far as the extremity of the Washburn group, and, after passing that, it turns north, with a very slight inclination west. The height of the plateau at the falls is about 7,800 feet. It increases slightly northeastward, until, in passing the mountains, it has an elevation of about 8,000 feet. Thence northward it decreases in height rapidly, and at the mouth of Tower Creek it reaches but 7,200 feet. At the head of the Upper Fall the river level is but a few feet below the top of the plateau. This fall adds 112, and the Lower Fall 300, feet to the depth of the chasm. From the foot of this fall to the mouth of East Fork the total fall is 1,304 feet in a distance of 24 miles, being an average of 54.3 feet per mile. As far as the extremity of the Washburn Mountains, a distance of twelve miles, the cañon continues to increase in depth, both by the fall of the stream and the rise of the plateau, and the extreme depth, 1,200 feet, is attained at this point. Thence the depth decreases rapidly, and at the mouth of Tower Creek it is but 500 or 600 feet deep on the west side, and about 1,000 feet on the east side. The width of the cañon at the top ranges from one-fourth of a mile to one mile, and the angle of slope of the walls from the top to the water's edge ranges from 45° to 75° with a horizontal line.

"The Yellowstone receives several tributaries from each side in its progress down the cañon. From the east, Jasper, Agate, Broad and Orange Creeks come in, and from the west a number of small streams, heading in the Washburn Mountains. As is usually the case in a land of cañons, these branches have much less erosive power than the main stream, and consequently reach it at a much higher level, necessitating a very rapid slope at the end or an abrupt fall. Many of these streams make very fine falls in reaching the cañon walls. This is particularly the case with the little streams on the west. They flow on the surface of the plateau, with a very gentle current, and have to make the whole descent to the bed of the cañon in a small fraction of a mile. The streams from the east, which head high up in the Amethyst Ridge, have long courses, and drain large areas. These streams cut cañons of considerable depth before they reach the main stream."

There are two good bridle-paths leading over Mount Washburn and past Tower Falls to Baronette's Bridge, connecting at that point with the wagon road from Cooke City to Mammoth Hot Springs. This is a favorite route with tourists accustomed to the saddle. It affords, from the summit of Mount Washburn, one of the most extensive and magnificent views in the Rocky Mountains, and is entirely free from difficulty or danger.

ROAD TO THE LAKE.

Retracing our road a short distance we follow up the Yellowstone River along the hill-side and through the timber. From several points, as we look back, a fine view of Mt. Washburn and the Yellowstone River may be had. The vivid reflections of the mountain upon the swift-flowing river, and the distinctness with which it may be seen in this clear atmosphere, lead one to believe that the mountain is but a mile away. At any time trout of wondrous size may be seen as we look down into the crystal waters, and every pebble upon the river's bottom is seen with surprising distinctness. Ducks and geese may be seen at any time along the gravelly bars, and pelican, as they lazily swim away from us, seem more than content with their dinner of Yellowstone trout. The road crosses Alum and Sour creeks, tributaries of the Yellowstone, and three miles from the Upper Falls we come to Sulphur Mountain.

Crater Hills.—These hills, sometimes known as Sulphur Mountain, consist of a group of detached hills or buttes, each about 150 feet in height, composed of the usual calcareous matter, largely impregnated with sulphur and iron. There are numerous sulphur springs at the foot of these hillocks, and also spouting from the pine-fringed plateau of a few acres in extent immediately about them. The deposits of sulphur are very pure, and there are great heaps of it in bright yellow crystals, amounting to hundreds of tons. The fumes are quite powerful and disagreeable. Much caution is to be advised in passing between the jets of steam which dart out of the ground near the verge of the seething caldrons. A horseman recently rode too near one of the pools, and the animal, in his terror, broke the crust, releasing a column of sulphur vapor which was almost overpowering. The escape of horse and rider from a horrible death was very narrow. No better description of these remarkable mounds could be given than that made by Lieut. Gustavus C. Doane, U. S. A., in his report of the Yellowstone Expedition of 1870. He said:

"I climbed to the summit of the two loftiest of these hills. Their formation is identical, all being composed of calcareous matter, solid within, but shelly on the exterior, and when decomposed, of a snowy whiteness. The slopes were covered with shales, slid down from above. On the summits were ruins of craters of great size and former solidity, now choked up with *debris*. From hydrostatic pressure all the springs had burst out below at the foot of the slopes, but through innumerable small vents all over the surface of the hills hot sulphur vapor escaped, subliming around the vents in splendid crystals of large size. The rocks were everywhere warm, and in some places hot to the touch; wherever the horses' feet broke through the crust, hot vapor escaped. Everywhere the rocks gave forth a hollow sound beneath our tread, and in many places the intense heat caused them to bulge out in a scaly formation, which broke through on the slightest pressure of the foot, whereupon scalding vapor poured out in such volumes as to cause a hasty retreat. The greatest spring in appearance lies at the base of the highest hill, and is intensely sulphurous, great clouds of vapor constantly escaping. It measures fifteen by twenty feet on the inside; the water boils up constantly from three to seven feet in height, the whole surface rising and falling occasionally with a flux and reflux of four feet additional, overflowing its basin and receding every few minutes. The basin is built up with a solid rim or lining of pure crystalline sulphur, four feet in width all round the edge, probably amounting to forty tons in weight. The water is clear, but of a whitish cast, and above the boiling point, steam being evolved from its surface. The basin can not be approached nearer than 20 feet distant on account of the scalding vapors. A small channel leads down the slope, and for several hundred feet its bed is encrusted with a sulphur deposit, showing that the spring occasionally flows a considerable quantity of water. This deposit is from three to ten inches deep. Farther along the base of the same hill is a sulphurous cavern of twenty feet in visible depth and eight feet in diameter, out of which issued jets of vapor with a sound like the puffing of a high-pressure steamboat. These jets pulsate regularly, and the vapor is intensely hot. Scattered along the bases of the next hills near by were great numbers of small sulphur springs of the same character and deposits as the larger one, any one of which would be counted a great curiosity in any district but this. About one hundred yards below is a spring of slate-colored water, seventy by thirty feet, an immense caldron, boiling constantly. Still farther on is a basin of perhaps four acres, containing from twenty to thirty mud springs, varying from two to twenty feet in diameter, and of depths below the surface from three to eight feet. The mud ejected is of different degrees of consistency, but generally about the thickness of common mortar, and mostly of an iron-brown color. It boils slowly, like mush, with bubbles of gas escaping, and is spouted to various heights from two to forty feet, falling with dull splashes around the edges of the craters, which are being built up continually, and continually caving in, to be worked over and ejected as before. Some of the springs throw up yellow mud, others white, and a few pink. The different springs of all classes had no apparent connection with each other, though often but a few feet apart, the mud being of different colors, the basins having different levels, and the pulsations being independent, one being frequently in violent ebullition, while another near by was quiescent. A plasterer would go into ecstacies over this mortar, which is worked to such a degree of fineness that it can be dried in large lumps, either in the sun or in a fire, without a sign of cracking, and when once dry is a soft, finely grained stone, resembling clay slate when dark, or meerschaum when white. Mortar might well be good after being constantly worked for, perhaps, ten thousand years. In a ravine near by was a large flowing spring of alum water, and several of sulphate of copper. Springs of this latter class are always clear and deep, with beautiful basins, raised slightly at the rim, and lined with encrustations of brilliant colors. Scattered over the whole area of one-fourth of a mile in diameter, in addition to the above, were hundreds of small spouts of vapor, water and mud. In a basin by itself was a black mud spring, twenty by forty feet, throwing mortar a distance of seventy feet; this substance was so strongly impregnated with sulphuric acid as to burn the tongue like fire in its intense sourness. All the mud springs are double, and most of the water springs also, each one having, in addition to its crater, and generally in the margin thereof, or near it, a honeycomb vent in the ground, or rock, through which the sulphur vapor escapes with a frying sound,— doubtless a vent for the internal fires below. This rule applies in all localities in the basin. The amount of pure crystalline sulphur deposited in this locality is very great ; probably 100 tons could be gathered in sight on the surface. The continuous supply will one day be turned to account in the manufacture of acids on a large scale."

The principal mud spring in this sub-group, the "Blue Mud Pot," is graphically described by Dr. Hayden, as follows:

"One of them has a basin 20 feet in diameter, nearly circular in form, and the contents have almost the consistency of thick hasty pudding. The surface is covered all over with puffs of mud, which, as they burst, give off a thud-like noise, and then the fine mud recedes from the centre of the puffs in the most perfect rings to the side. This mud-pot presents this beautiful picture ; and, although there are hundreds of them, yet it is very rare that the mud is in just the condition to admit of these peculiar rings. The kind of thud is, of course, produced by the escape of the sulphureted hydrogen gas through the mud. Indeed, there is no comparison that can bring before the mind a clearer picture of such a mud volcano than a huge caldron of thick mush. The mud is so fine as to have no visible or sensible grain, and is very strongly impregnated with alum. For 300 yards in length and 25 yards in width the valley of this little branch of Alum Creek is perforated with these mud-vents of all sizes, and the contents are of all degrees of consistency, from merely turbid water to a thick mortar. The entire surface is perfectly bare of vegetation, and hot; yielding in many places to a slight pressure.

YELLOWSTONE LAKE ROAD.

Two miles from Sulphur Mountain the forks of the road are reached. The course of the river is continuously followed southward from the forks of the road for eight miles, through a beautiful valley, with picturesque views of small islands in the stream, of high mountains and long stretches of woodland. On the way there are also many hot springs to be seen. These are always pleasant to look upon, as constantly presenting new instances of Nature's wayward moods.

Mud Geyser and Belching Spring.—These are situated in a wooded ravine a short distance to the right of the road, attracting attention by their noisiness and columns of vapor. The most terrible geyser in this group has been inactive for a few years past. Its crater, forty-five by seventy-five feet, is still to be seen. But there are several wonderful objects of interest left, an inspection of which ought not to be omitted. The most curious is the Mud Geyser. This is a cavern on the slope of the hill. It has a crater thirty feet in diameter at the verge, which is slightly elevated at the lower side, and hemmed in by the hill on the upper. This yawning crater narrows as it deepens to about fifteen feet at the lowest visible point, thirty feet below. Great volumes of steam escape, ascending high into the air. There is a rumbling sound in regular beats of a few seconds' interval, and a jarring of the earth for some distance around, after which comes a great surging of the slate-colored mud horizontally out of the orifice under the cliff, beating itself furiously into spray against the walls of the deep crater, which soon fills nearly to the top. The pasty mud is then sucked back with horrible groanings into the vent, utterly disappearing from sight, only to be again belched forth with renewed rumblings and earth vibrations, perhaps in greater volume than at first. This is an appalling sight; but it is very fascinating, nevertheless. The spectator is constantly in expectation that these violent throes of the volcano will be increased to that degree that the tall trees on the hillside will be splashed by the mud. Indeed, they are coated with it; but upon this point Dr. Peale reports:

"Last year, when at this locality, we noticed that the trees had their branches coated with mud, and the question was raised as to how the mud got there; we concluded that the geyser sometimes ejected its contents. This year, however, investigation seemed to prove that the mud is carried up mechanically, mixed with the steam that is constantly rising from the caldron, and that the spring never has any eruptions. We were led to this opinion first by noticing that it was only the under side of the branches that held the mud. Mr. Holmes then placed some dead branches in such a position that the steam came upon them, and in a few hours they had a coating of mud. Again, some of the trees of which the branches are coated are living, which would hardly be the case had they received the mud from an eruption. Again, reason also is found in the fact that the surface of the spring is constantly agitated, which is rarely or never the case with a true geyser. Still, in the past it may have been a geyser, and had regular eruptions."

About twenty rods distant northward from the Mud Geyser is another large boiling spring of crystalline water, called the

Crater Hills, Mud Geyser, and Hot Springs, or Yellowstone Lake.

"Grotto," sending off volumes of sulphurous vapor. It is very curious in its operation, eructating at intervals with a loud belch, filling its basin to the brim, its pulsations shaking the ground. It then suddenly draws the water in again with a tremendous gurgle, repeating the process *ad infinitum*. The opening is three feet high, eight feet wide and about twenty feet deep. The entrance is somewhat like a Gothic arch, and the walls within and without are stained in various shades of bright green by the mineral constituents of the water. Near this point in 1877 the Nez Percé Indians crossed the river, hotly pursued by the gallant Howard and his troops. It has since been known as the Nez Percé ford. Remains of the breastworks behind which Chief Joseph entrenched himself for a time are still visible.

The Yellowstone Lake.—This large and beautiful sheet of water lies in the lap of snow-capped mountains at an elevation of 7,788 feet above the sea. Its peculiar shape, rudely representing that of the opened palm of the right hand, particularly when looked down upon from an adjacent height, has fixed the name of the Thumb and Fingers upon the bays, separated by long and narrow peninsulas, which indent its southern and western sides. Its dimensions are about twenty miles north and south, and fifteen miles across the thumb and palm, its area being 150 square miles. Its depth is so great that soundings a short distance from its banks have not been reached with 225 feet of line. It is the largest lake at a great elevation in North America, although many lakes in Colorado are from 2,000 to 3,000 feet higher. Even Shoshone Lake, in the Park, exceeds the elevation of its grander neighbor by eighty feet, and Lake Carpenter, in the Big Horn Mountains, is at least 3,000 feet higher. That the elevation of the Yellowstone Lake is, however, enormous, may be illustrated by the fact that if Mount Washington, in New Hampshire, the highest peak in the Eastern States, could be sunk in this large body of water, with its base at the sea level, its apex would be nearly half a mile below the surface of the lake. The sources of the Yellowstone River are in the Yellowstone Mountains, perhaps fifty miles distant from the lake, and the latter is only a widening of this stream, which enters the extremity of the little finger at the south, and discharges at the wrist at the north. The lake receives few tributaries of great size. By far the largest are Beaver Dam Creek and Pelican Creek, both on the eastern side. Besides these, there are a score of small streams from the encircling mountains, some of which are strongly charged with minerals. This fact, in connection with the sulphur, alum and alkali springs which not only dot the shores of the lake, but boil up from its depths at many points, renders the water at some places near the banks warm and murky. But, as a general statement, the lake is of crystal clearness, the average temperature being 60° F., and the purity and sweetness of the water leave nothing to be desired. Strong westerly winds prevail every afternoon, ruffling the surface of the water, and sometimes causing a heavy surf to dash upon the beach.

As to the enchanting loveliness of the lake, there can only be one opinion. Its varied charms surpass those of the famous inland seas of the Alps. Toward the east and south the mountains, rugged, gray and cold, with snowy peaks and grand crags sharply outlined against the sky, come down abruptly to the flood, by which they are reflected as in a mirror. On the west are low bluffs fringed with timber, and an occasional densely wooded island, upon which the eye rests gratefully as it takes in the dazzling glories of the scene. Stephenson's, Frank's, and some of the other islands are only slightly elevated above the surface of the lake, the shores of which are broken by bays and inlets, the strand glistening and flashing in the sunlight with bright pebbles and crystals and bits of obsidian. Especially is this the case on the north-eastern shore. In one locality, called Concretion Cove, which is a prolongation of Mary's Bay, between the mouth of Pelican Creek and Steamboat Point, the beach is shingled with the most curious specimens of indurated clays and shales and fossils. The concretions are remarkable for the brilliancy of their colors, and the singularity of their forms. Some resemble shoe soles, stockings, pot-lids, rolling pins, pestles, ladles, cups, pitchers, lather-boxes and divers other things. The lather-boxes are very uniform in color, size, shape and banding, at first glance seeming like lathe-work, and they may be easily split along the lines of stratification. One of the peculiarities of the Yellowstone Lake country, and one which it shares with the Hoodoo Region, hereafter described, consists in the low rumbling sounds that are frequently heard immediately overhead. This remarkable phenomenon, entitled to rank among the greatest wonders of this world of marvels, appears entirely to have escaped the notice of the scientific men who have visited the Park. It is probably due to an atmospheric disturbance caused by the violent eruptions and the liberation of gases constantly going on in the Park; but it is impossible to overlook the fact that it occurs only in localities far removed from the most violent manifestations of energy.

Yellowstone Lake Trout.—The lake is entirely destitute of all fish save trout. These, however, are so plentiful at almost every point along the shores, that there is little sport afforded in capturing them. They are large, and voracious in the extreme, particularly for grasshoppers, and two men could catch them faster than six men could get them ready for the cook. In a number of localities it is quite easy for the angler to land his fish and drop it in a boiling pool behind him, without changing his position or even unhooking his victim. Whether he will eat his trout after it is cooked is somewhat questionable. Unfortunately, most of these fish, as well as

Yellowstone Lake.

those caught in the river above the Upper Falls, are infested with long, slender white worms, which not only breed in the intestines, but burrow into the flesh. Col. Norris, late Superintendent of the Park, in writing of this peculiarity, affirms that all the trout of the cold-water tributaries of the river below the lake to the first rapids contain these parasites. This point he has fully established by experiment, indicating that the cause of the presence of the worms exists in the lake. Beyond this no theory to account for the phenomenon is hazarded. Col. Norris thinks it can not be due to the quantities of minute vegetable substances which are often thrown up in windrows along the rocky shores, and discolor the otherwise clear water, because several other lakes, famous for excellent trout, are not only excessively weedy, but are impregnated with minerals to a far greater degree than the Yellowstone Lake; besides, nowhere else is the trout in finer condition than in the main Yellowstone near Tower Falls, and thence beyond to its confluence with the East Fork, and up the latter where the sulphur fumes arising from the water are so powerful as to be almost unendurable. Nor are the fish found to be affected injuriously which are taken in Soda Butte and Cache Creeks, branches of the East Fork, although they frequent waters the rocky channels of which are coated with the sulphur deposits of many boiling springs. Prof. Leidy calls this worm *Dibothrium cordiceps*, and says it is found in little sacs imbedded in the flesh. He considers it entirely different from the worms found in the European salmon. But it is not a constant parasite of the trout, as perfectly healthy specimens are often caught, which show on their scarred bodies the places where their tormentors have burrowed through. The infested trout are notably plentiful in the lake at the locality where the Shoshone trail leaves it, and where the water bubbles with hot gases.

Hot Springs on Yellowstone Lake.—This place is

called Hot Spring Camp. Here is to be seen a large and most interesting system of boiling springs, which no visitor should fail to examine. There are small geysers, steam jets, paint pots, and an infinite variety of hot springs. This remarkable locality may well be regarded as the Park museum, where specimens of all the various kinds of formation to be found may be seen. In amazement at these wonders, the magnificent and romantic scenery of the lake is apt to be disregarded. The first most noticeable object is the high crater of a calcareous spring, situated on the very verge of the water. From this a boiling stream is poured into the cold and limpid flood. There are other craters, built partly in and partly out of the lake; while at some distance from the strand the eye rests upon deep, dark caverns, easily distinguishable from the surrounding shallows, out of the depths of which streams of gas-bubbles are constantly rushing to the surface. On a gentle slope extending along the shore of the lake for over a mile and reaching far back into the woods, are flowing springs of all sizes, shapes and colors. Some of the pools are from thirty to seventy feet in length, and from fifteen to forty feet in width. The water is apparently fathomless, and of indescribable translucency. Convulsive throbbings, accompanied by clouds of vapor, are constant. The largest springs are a turquoise blue, others are emerald; still others are pure white, while some are red and other hues. The craters of all these various fountains are lined with a silvery white deposit which illuminates, by reflection, the perpendicular but irregular walls to an immense depth. Indeed, it would seem that objects hundreds of feet down in the crystalline abysses are distinctly visible. An anomalous feature of this wonderful hot spring system is that pools of different colors lie in closest proximity, each spring being independent of the other, having varying levels at the surface, as well as varying temperatures and pulsations. While some of the pools are in halcyon repose, others are angrily boiling. The fretwork formations on the sides and rims of the craters are exquisitely beautiful. No possible description could convey the faintest idea of the opulence of coloring, nor of the variety and delicacy of the deposits. Some of the latter seem to be as fragile as the down on a butterfly's wing, and as evanescent to the touch; while others, particularly the silicious, are as hard as adamant. Seldom are the water and deposits of any two springs alike. There are coral, honeycomb, brainstone, pebble, scale and crystal formations, the whole making kaleidoscopic groupings of color and design. Down in the limpid depths of many of the springs are grottoes and arch-like structures. One dazzling white pool, the very type of purity, entrances the visitor, who stands with wondering eyes to look far down below upon what may only be likened to a resplendent fairy grotto of frosted silver encrusted with pearls. Another crystal-clear and colorless basin has a rim blazing with hues of sapphire, opal, ruby and emerald. Still another pool, full to the brim, has the corrugated sides of its profound deeps adorned with tints of reddish gold. Several basins of unknown depth are mantled with a saffron scum of the consistency of calf's leather. This undulates sluggishly with the water, giving the pools the appearance of a tanner's vat. This leathery substance is not of a vegetable nature, but is deposited by the mineral constituents of the springs. It forms in layers, which are brightly mottled with red, yellow, green and black on the under surface, and the lowermost strata are solidified into pure, finely grained sheets resembling alabaster. There are hundreds of springs in this system, each, if possible, more wonderful than the other. The shallow channels by which their overflow is carried off to the lake are gorgeously tinted, and even the shale of the beach is mottled red, yellow, green and black. These bright colors are, however, only on the surface of the rock, soon fading away when the specimens become dry. The marvels of this hot spring area amaze and confound the beholder, the reality surpassing the most vivid imagination of scenes of enchantment.

A terrace of calcareous stalagmite, from twenty to fifty feet in depth, runs along the shore of the lake for a considerable distance, the edges of which are worn to a bluff bank by the action of the water. In riding along, other springs as remarkable as those which have been left, are seen near the trail. Some of them are noticed in the lake itself, a few rods from the shore, the dark depths of the craters showing in striking contrast with the shallow water on the shelving beach.

Paint Pots on the Lake.—Not far beyond is a very fine collection of paint pots. These are situated about 400 yards from the shore, covering a space not more than half an acre in extent, but forming a system of themselves. Attention is at first attracted by irregular mounds of pink earth as high as the breastworks of rifle pits. Approaching nearer, a group of small conical craters, surrounding a seething basin of pink slime, is found. Most of the small craters are in violent activity, sputtering and casting up clots of mud. These paint pots are noticeable for the exquisitely soft tints of their paste-like contents. The shades of color embrace pearl gray, lavender, pale pink, glowing crimson, green, orange, pure white and white with a tint of blue. Some of the throats of the craters are as smooth as those of porcelain pitchers, and have lips as finely curved. The deposit hardens into a firm, laminated clay stone of fine texture, though here, as elsewhere in the Park, the colors lose their brilliancy as the substance cools and dries.

Other Hot Spring Groups.—There are numerous other groups of springs on the shores of the lake, among which may be named Sulphur Hill Springs, on the north side, consisting of a mass of deposit 600 feet along the shore, and 400 feet in thickness. These springs are mainly extinct. A very large group of all sizes and varieties of springs is found at Turbid

Lake, two miles from Steamboat Point. The name Steamboat Point was suggested by the fact that on the point of the bluff, which here extends into the northeast corner of the lake, there is a powerful vent, from which the steam escapes in a vast column with a continuous roar similar to the noise made by a steamship when blowing off steam. At the northeast corner of Mary's Bay, about two miles from Steamboat Point, is another chain of springs, most of them bubbling, and depositing a lead-colored substance. Near the shore on the east side of the beautiful bay, south of Steamboat Point, at Lake Butte, is still another group of hot springs and steam jets. On the northwestern slope of the ridge that extends southwest from Mount Stevenson, about a mile east of the lake, is an area of spring deposits about three miles in extent. This is called Brimstone Basin. It is easily seen from a distance, the white deposits on the slopes rendering it conspicuous, the sulphurous odors greeting the visitor long before he reaches the place. But all these springs, interesting as they doubtless are, would scarcely repay the tourist for the time and trouble necessary to reach them, particularly as they present no special peculiarities in comparison with the various groups that lie within the range of routes that are more accessible.

Should Congress grant the necessary appropriation, it is proposed to construct a road from Upper Geyser Basin via Shoshone Lake to the West Thumb of Yellowstone Lake, and thence to the outlet of Yellowstone Lake; also to construct a road from Grand Cañon over Mount Washburn to Mammoth Hot Springs, thus completing the circuit of the Park, and enabling tourists to traverse it from one end to the other, without doubling back over the same road. This will add greatly to the attractiveness of the trip throughout.

At present, unless the tourist wishes to cross the Shoshone trail to the Upper Geyser Basin, he must retrace the route to the forks of the road. Following the left-hand road for some seven miles brings him to Trout and Alum creeks. Alum Creek and Violet Creek, one of its small branches, have their origin in two important groups of hot springs in the water-shed between the Madison and Yellowstone rivers. The head of Violet Creek is a semicircular basin, bounded by a low hill, bare on the sides and wooded at the summit. To look down into this basin from the top of the hill is like looking into a volcanic crater. All through it there are scattered fumaroles, solfatari, and mud springs, some of the latter showing blue and violet colors.

Sulphur Lake and Alum Creek.—Ascending the Eastern slope of the divide, the odor of sulphur gives warning that another group of springs is near. There are numerous hot springs at intervals, and jets of steam force their way with a hissing and rumbling sound through the glaring white masses of deposit, while the animals are compelled to pick their steps gingerly over the frequent rivulets of scalding water which cross the road in their flow into Alum Creek, an important tributary of the Yellowstone, the banks of which are riddled by hundreds of boiling and bubbling springs of varied character, and the water of the stream is so highly impregnated that animals will not touch it.

Following the road up over the divide, past Mary's Lake and over Mary's Mountain, we come rather abruptly to the Westward slope. From the mountain-side a panorama of beautiful forest and mountain scenery is unfolded, the view from the highest point being so extended that the great part of the Western mountain ranges, which bound the spacious Park, may be seen in all their magnificence and majesty.

Descending the divide we follow down the valley of the East Fork of the Firehole River. This large stream, fed by hot springs, presents peculiar and interesting features of its own. It heads in the divide between the Yellowstone and Madison rivers, opposite Alum Creek. It has many branches, with short, steep courses, which collect in a basin at the foot of the divide, whence the stream pursues a course nearly West, down a narrow valley, between high walls. Heavy pine grow along its banks, and here and there a little meadow in its numerous bends. After fording the river a number of times the valley widens and we come to the Lower Geyser Basin.

THE LOWER GEYSER BASIN.

This Basin is a wide valley, extending southward from the junction of the East Fork of the Firehole River with the main stream. The area covered by the entire Basin is between thirty and forty square miles, over which the springs are scattered in groups. Of these springs, Dr. Hayden's survey has catalogued 693, exclusive of seventeen geysers. The central portion of the valley is a flat plain, six or seven miles in width, partially timbered, but mainly bare, and covered with either spring deposits or marsh.

"In some of the elements of beauty and interest," says Professor R. W. Raymond, "the Lower Geyser Basin is superior to its more startling rival. It is broader and more easily surveyed as a whole, and its springs are more numerous, though not so powerful. Nothing can be lovelier than the sight, at sunrise, of the white steam columns, tinged with rosy morning, ascending against the background of the dark pine woods and the clear sky above. The variety in form and character of these springs is quite remarkable. A few of them make faint deposits of sulphur, though the greater number appear to be purely silicious. One very large basin (forty by sixty feet) is filled with the most beautiful slime, varying in tint from white to pink, which blobs and spits away, trying to boil, like a heavy theologian forcing a laugh to please a friend, in spite of his natural specific gravity. * * * * The extinct geysers are the most beautiful objects of all. Around their borders the white encrustations form quaint arabesques and ornamental bosses, resembling petrified vegetable growths. The sides of the reservoir are corrugated and indented fancifully, like the recesses and branching passages of a fairy cavern. The water is brightly but not deeply blue. Over its surface curls a light vapor; through its crystal clearness one may gaze, apparently to unfathomable depths; and, seen through this wondrous medium, the white walls seem like silver, ribbed and crusted with pearl. When the sun strikes across the scene, the last touch of unexpected beauty is added. The projected shadow of the decorated edge reveals by contrast new glories in the depths ; every ripple on the surface makes marvelous play of tint and shade on the pearly bottom. One half expects to see a lovely naiad emerge with floating grace from her fantastically carven covert, and gayly kiss her snowy hand through the blue wave. In one of these *laugs* the whitened skeleton of a mountain buffalo was discovered. By whatever accident he met his fate there, no king or saint was ever more magnificently entombed. Not the shrine of St. Antony of Padua, with its white marbles and its silver lamps, is so resplendent as this sepulchre in the wilderness."

The general elevation of the Basin is 7,252 feet, and above this the surrounding plateau rises from 400 to 800 feet, the slopes being heavily timbered. The first interesting group of springs to be noticed lie at the foot of the bluffs, concealed from view by the trees. Some of them are of great beauty. One is a white cavern, from which the water bubbles over black pebbles. Another is a white mud-pot. A third is a beautiful white basin with cliff-like sides, the water clear and tinted blue. There are thirty-six springs in this group, but no geysers.

The Thud Group.—About half a mile distant from the camp, southward along the edge of the timber, are the Thud Springs, covering an area of about sixteen acres, and fronting the open portion of the Basin. There are many interesting springs in this group, most of which have circular basins widening below the surface, with overhanging rims. The Stirrup Spring, eight by nine feet, is said to resemble the head of an old woman, with a cap on, the scalloped edge of the spring representing the ruffles, the fissure the mouth, and two steam vents the eyes. The Fungoid Spring, one of the thudders, is named from the peculiar fungoid-like masses which form its rim. West of this spring, 140 feet, is a basin, measuring sixteen by eighteen feet, and varying in depth from eight to thirteen feet, with orifices so deep that they can not be measured. This spring seems to have three centres of ebullition, two of which are quite active. At intervals of a few minutes, there is an accumulation of steam, the escape of which, with a muffled thud, shakes the ground. The water is of an inky green color, and has a temperature of about 187° F. Another spring has the rim of its basin ornamented with a formation that looks something like oak leaves. The wealth of colors, and the forms of the deposits about this group, are remarkable.

The Fountain Geyser.—This Geyser is the most important known in the Basin. It is situated in the midst of a group of smaller geysers, springs and mud-pots, about a quarter of a mile south of the Thud Group. It consists of a spring, thirty feet in length by twenty in width, which is separated by a narrow constriction from a surrounding pool 120 by 100 feet in dimensions. This spring is situated on a broad and conspicuous table-like mound, the edge of which forms a distinct rim around the basin, over which it projects a few inches. The sides of the spring slope inward in somewhat rounded masses, which are distinctly seen when the water is low in the basin, and resemble a series of cushions around the edge. In the centre of the spring is the geyser tube. The rim marks the level at which the water usually stands, and just outside of this, on three sides, there are irregular, mound-like masses of beaded geyserite from two to four feet in height. In one end of the basin is the tube of the geyser, over which the water is of a wonderfully blue color. The pool around the spring is generally shallow, and without a marked rim. It has two basins or bowls, however, that are deep. The largest of these is about fifty feet in diameter, with greenish tinted water. This geyser operates about once in four hours, and continues spasmodically in action, sometimes for sixty minutes. Dr. Peale wrote: "The spouting occurs from the crater-like hole, and, preceding action, the water was boiling vigorously, somewhat like the Giantess, in the Upper Basin. A great mass of water was pushed out tumultuously to an average height of about ten feet, and through this jets were projected which reached a maximum height of fifty feet. There appeared to be several centres from which the steam escaped, and the water was churned and dashed about until it was a white mass. There were periods of increased activity and cessation. About half an hour before the eruption, the water did not quite fill the basin; but, immediately after it was over, it was level with the top; eight minutes later it was six inches below the rim." West of the geyser, near the edge of the terrace, is a group of springs about which the ground appears to be deluged in blood, caused by Algæ, a low form of vegetable growth.

The Jet Geyser.—This geyser is a short distance south of the Fountain. Its beaded basin is twenty feet in diameter, sloping to a funnel, with an orifice at the bottom only about a foot in width. When the geyser is in action the basin fills, and the water is cast violently out in all directions, with an occasional perpendicular jet to a height of ten or fifteen feet. The water is greatly agitated, and its movement is accompanied by a throbbing noise beneath the surface. After an eruption is over the water sinks out of sight. This geyser is frequently in action.

The Mud Caldron or Mammoth Paint Pots.—A few rods eastward, on an eminence above the Fountain, from which it is separated by a fringe of trees, is a very large and curious mud caldron measuring about 40 by 60 feet, the rim on three sides of which is from four to five feet in height. The substance contained in this basin is a fine, white, pasty mass of silicious clay in constant agitation. There is a continual bursting of bubbles with a plop-plop like that of boiling mush. The mud rises in globular masses, cones, rings, and jets. At the south end of the basin the rim is low, and bounds an area the surface of which is cracked, and over which are grouped some thirty or forty cones or mud-puffs of most delicate shades of pink and rose color. These mud-puffs are two feet or more in height, and send out spurts four or five feet into the air, the paste or mud being much thicker than that in the main basin.

Other Geysers and Springs.—About half a mile a little south of east of the Mud Caldron, is an important group of springs and ponds, and a lake of hot water, from which a network of streamlets carries the overflow to the river. In this area are numbers of trees which have been killed by the hot water. There are several minor geysers in this group, among which may be named the Bead, the Pink Cone, the Steady, the Young Hopeful, Black Warrior, and the Gray Bulger. Not one of these is without curious and beautiful features that would be attractive to the visitor. But this group, as well as the White Dome Group, below mentioned, are seldom visited by the tourist. After crossing the wooded terraces which surround this group, and bearing somewhat south of west over difficult ground, cut up by rivulets and partly marshy, the banks of White Creek, a tributary of the Firehole, are reached. In this vicinity are many other springs and geysers. Among them is the White Dome Geyser, with a conspicuous, although crumbling and decayed, cone, twenty-five feet in height, resting on a platform of deposit.

This geyser steams vigorously and an occasional splash of water leads one to believe that it is gaining in activity. The cone is intensely warm and is covered with small steam-vents from which is escaping superheated steam. Not far southward is a very important geyser, called the Great Fountain, the bowl of which is on a platform of beautifully ornamented geyserite 120 feet in diameter. It sends out a mass of water, during eruption, in the utmost confusion, spreading out at every angle, and whirling in every direction, some jets rising vertically to the height of 150 feet, then separating into large, glistening drops, and falling back into the whirling mass of water and steam; others shooting at an angle of forty-five degrees, and falling upon the islands and pools thirty or forty feet from the base. The action of this geyser continues an hour, and occurs every twelve to twenty hours, presenting the view of a symmetrical fountain with a thousand jets which describe curves of almost equal length on all sides. Beauty Spring, across the creek, is remarkable for the vivid coloring of its deposits, which stain a large surrounding area with tints of rainbow brilliancy. These unique attractions of the Lower Geyser Basin should not be overlooked.

Returning from this round of the Lower Basin, and again resuming the journey, the wagon road winds southwestwardly over the plateau, crossing a number of rivulets in its course, and also Fountain Creek. Some hundred yards west of this stream, on both banks of the Firehole River, extending north as far as the mouth of Fairy Falls Creek, is still another large group of springs, very beautiful with respect to the transparency and colors of the water, and presenting an infinite variety in structure and ornamentation, but having no geysers of note.

Fairy Falls, Twin Domes and the Queen's Laundry. —The visitor is recommended, before entering upon an inspection of the Lower Geyser Basin, to make a trip to Fairy Falls, on the creek of that name, taking in at the same time some other points of interest in the vicinity. These are easily accessible by bridle-path from the forks of the Firehole River. There is a pleasant ride of two miles, mainly through the pine woods, then the valley opens, and two dome-like hills of symmetrical shape are seen in the midst of it. Each dome is crowned with a beautiful boiling spring, the rims of the basins being perfectly scalloped and ornamented. The water is blue as a sapphire, and, in coursing down the sloping sides of the mounds, paints them with brilliant colors. These mounds have been named the Twin Domes. The adjacent hills are the resort of bison and elk, large numbers of which come down the valleys to graze in the early spring. A quarter of a mile beyond is an extraordinary fountain of boiling water called the Queen's Laundry. It has a basin thirty by fifty feet in dimensions, whence its crystal waters overflow and descend by an extensive series of low terraces that are divided into innumerable small pools, which are partitioned by beautiful coral-like ridges into natural bath-tubs, a foot to four feet in depth, the sides of which are enameled in purest white. The water, which is exceedingly soft, gradually cools as it flows over each succeeding terrace, so that a bath may be taken at any desired temperature. A little further on, Fairy Falls Creek makes a direct leap of 250 feet over a cliff, amid surroundings which are charming in the extreme.

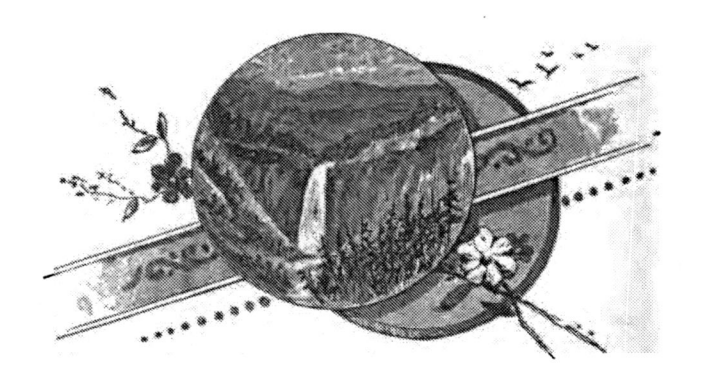

THE MIDWAY GEYSER BASIN.

From the Lower to the Upper Geyser Basin there are two roads, both following, in the main, the valley of the Firehole or Madison River, and affording an alternative route between the two points, which are only eleven miles apart. Midway between the two basins, and named from its geographical relation to them, is another important group of geysers and boiling springs. This group occupies an area which extends along the river about a mile in length and a quarter of a mile in width. The principal springs are found on a mound about fifty feet above the river level, on the left bank of the stream, at the lower or northern end of the group. Among them is the Excelsior Geyser, which is, doubtless, the largest geyser in the world. Although this group of springs is commonly designated the Middle Geyser Basin, it really should be classified with the springs of the Lower Basin, within the limits of which it is situated,—the cañon which separates the Lower Basin from the Upper Basin only beginning just above the southern boundary of the group. Dr. Peale has named these springs the " Half-way Group, or Egeria Springs."

The Excelsior Geyser.—This formidable geyser is the most powerful known to be in existence. The river intervenes between it and the road on the east side of the river; but it is accessible by the bridge a few rods northward. In 1871 it was thought to be an immense spring, and received the name of the Caldron from Dr. Hayden's party. In the report of the United States Geological Survey for that year it is thus described:

" It seems to have broken out close by the river, and to have continually enlarged its orifice by the breaking of its sides. It evidently commenced on the east side, and the continual wear of the under side of the crust on the west side has caused the margin to fall in until an aperture at least 250 feet in diameter has been formed, with walls or sides twenty to thirty feet high, showing the laminæ of deposition perfectly. The water is intensely agitated all the time, boiling like a caldron, from which a vast column of steam is ever arising, filling the orifice. As the passing breeze sweeps it away for a moment, one looks down into this terrible, seething pit with terror. All around the sides are large masses of the silicious crust that have fallen from the rim. An immense column of water flows out of this caldron into the river. As it pours over the marginal slope, it descends by numerous small channels, with a large number of smaller ones, spreading over a broad surface, and the marvelous beauty of the strikingly vivid coloring far surpasses anything of the kind we have seen in this land of wondrous beauty. There is every possible shade of color, from vivid scarlet to a bright rose, and every shade of yellow to delicate cream, mingled with vivid green from minute vegetation. Some of the channels were lined with a very fine, delicate, yellow, silky material, which vibrates at every movement of the waters."

In 1880 this geyser was noted by Dr. Peale as an immense pit, of rather irregular outline, 330 feet in length and 200 feet wide at the widest part, the water being of a deep blue tint, and intensely agitated all the time, dense clouds of steam constantly ascending from it. Only when the vapor is wafted aside by the breeze can the surface of the water, fifteen or twenty feet below the surrounding level, be seen. The walls are perpendicular, cliff-like, and sometimes overhang on three sides, but are worn away at the outlet by the immense volume of hot water which pours down the slope into the river. The deposit in which this spring is cut is laminated old spring deposits, showing that the spring is secondary in its formation. It is probable, that, when the laminated deposit was laid down, the spring on the summit was the principal spring, and of vastly greater extent.

"It appears," writes the authority before named, "that this spring broke out near the river, and has been working backward, the constant undermining of the deposits continually enlarging the basin of the spring. Large masses have broken off the edge and have tumbled in. Toward the river the walls become less high, as the top has the slope of the mound, which is in that direction. There is an immense column of water pouring from the spring, which soon spreads out on terraces, and finally pours over the marginal slope in two well-defined channels. Some of the upper channels are small and narrow, and others broad, all brilliantly colored, yellow, orange, red and rose tints being liberally displayed on a white ground. It was impossible to obtain the temperature in the central portion of the basin. In the outlet the water had a temperature of 175 degrees F. This was taken on the terraces above the deeper channels, and was, of course, lower than the actual temperature of the spring. Around the outside of the pit, or caldron, a pile of *debris* composed of broken pieces of geyserite, was seen, forming a sort of rim, just as though it had been washed back by an overflow of the spring. This, however, I think is impossible, on account of the absence of a wall at the foot of the spring. It is possible that it may be a geyser with long periods; but we have no data to that effect."

In the fall of 1881 the Excelsior revealed itself as a stupendous geyser. Colonel Norris asserts that he at first heard its spoutings at a point six miles distant, but reached the scene too late to witness them, although he saw the effects of the eruption upon the Firehole River, which was so swollen by the flood as to wash away some bridges over the small streams below. In February, 1882, the Excelsior became frightfully violent in its eruptions, causing the earth to rumble, and filling the valley with dense vapor. The period of action began about 10 P. M., gradually becoming later every night, until, on the first of July, the eruption took place at 10 A. M., showing a loss of twelve hours during nine months. It is reported that in the summer of 1882 the power of the eruptions was almost incredible, " elevating sufficient water to heights of from 100 to 300 feet to render the Firehole River, here nearly 100 yards wide, a foaming torrent of steaming hot water, and hurling rocks of from one to one hundred pounds in weight, like those from an exploded mine, over surrounding acres." From this time until about March, 1888, the Excelsior remained inactive; notwithstanding many false reports to the contrary.

The Excelsior has increased in activity ever since, giving two or more displays daily, sending out a compact body of water from sixty to seventy-five feet in diameter to a height varying from 60 to 250 feet. It is a sufficiently awe-inspiring experience, as the writer can affirm, to stand at the verge of this steaming lake, upon the hollow crust which projects over the boiling water, and peer down upon the agitated surface as the clouds of scalding vapor are occasionally lifted by the breeze. But when this geyser is in action, the awful noise and concussion produced by the falling water, accompanied by rumblings and vibrations like those of an earthquake, and the disagreeable habit of vomiting up stones, which is a special characteristic, warrant the visitor in keeping a safe distance away during the display of its terrible power.

Grand Prismatic Spring.—Perhaps the very largest, and certainly one of the most beautiful springs in the Park, is that called the Grand Prismatic Spring. It is situated a short distance west of the Excelsior Geyser, its dimensions being 250 by 350 feet. It was named on account of the brilliant tints of the water. Unfortunately, the clouds of steam which are constantly arising from the surface of this basin greatly obscure the view; but a good point of observation is from the bluff on the opposite side of the river. Over the central pit or bowl the water is deep blue in color, changing into green toward the edge. The water of the shallower surrounding basin is of a yellow tint, fading into orange. Outside the rim there is a brilliant red deposit, which shades into purples, browns and grays, all painted upon a ground of grayish white which forms the mound, built up of layers of silicious deposit, upon which the spring is situated. These colors are in vivid bands, which are strikingly marked and distinct. The water flowing off in every direction, with constant wave-like pulsations, over the beautifully scalloped and slightly raised rim of the spring, has formed a succession of terraces, a few inches in height, down the slopes of the mound, especially on the southern face. The depth and richness of the colors around this spring can not be exaggerated. The temperature of the water at the north end near the edge is about 146° F. Not far to the northward of the spring just described is another with dark blue water, called the Turquoise. It measures 100 by 100 feet. Its overflow is carried off by a channel two feet wide and eight inches deep, the bottom of which is a brilliant white, and the edges yellow, fading into salmon color as the river is approached.

On either side of the road from this point onward, especially on the left bank of the river, are numerous other springs, and an occasional small geyser. But the tourist, unless he have an abundance of time at his disposal, will scarcely linger to inspect them. About the centre of the Middle Geyser Basin group, there is a sharp bend of the river to the east as it comes from the wooded cañon above. The new road from Upper Geyser Basin crosses the river at this point upon a substantial bridge. Half a mile beyond this point a hot flood, from an extensive system of springs on Rabbit Branch, is poured into the stream, the banks of which all along its course, until the Upper Geyser Basin is reached, five miles further, are pitted with springs, while the inclosing hills are flecked with fleecy clouds of steam which rise out of the forest. Indeed, the river in this part of its career, receives so much hot water that the visitor is likely to think the name Firehole has been aptly bestowed upon it.

THE UPPER GEYSER BASIN.

The principal geysers of the Park, which are also the most powerful in the world, are in this Basin, which extends from Old Faithful down the main Firehole River, to a point just below the mouth of the Little Firehole River, and along Iron Spring Creek, a branch of the last-named stream. The more important springs and geysers are on the main river. As the Firehole and Little Firehole Rivers converge as they flow northward, the Basin is almost triangular in shape. The extent of the Basin is about four square miles; but the chief geysers are situated within an area of perhaps half a mile, along the course of the Firehole, on either side of the stream. This flows from southeast to northwest through the Basin, taking a more northerly course, however, after the waters of Iron Spring Creek and the Little Firehole unite with it. The volume of the Firehole is sometimes greatly increased, just after the eruption of some of the larger geysers, and the temperature of the water is affected by the springs. For example, in the distance of a quarter of a mile from Old Faithful, to a point opposite the Grand Geyser, the river has been found 7° Fahrenheit warmer. The surface of the Basin consists of a succession of ridges and knolls, crowned with geysers and boiling springs. On every side are mountains, 1,500 feet or more in height, the slopes of which are heavily timbered, although there are occasional outcroppings of rough basaltic rocks among the pines. Clouds of steam hang as a pall over the Basin, and columns of vapor float upward like water wraiths from between the tree-tops of the surrounding forest. The earth is full of rumbling and gurgling sounds, and the air is laden with sulphurous fumes. Stupendous fountains of boiling water, veiled in spray, shoot toward heaven, at varying heights, like cascades reversed, glinting and coruscating and scintillating in the sunlight, until their force is expended, when they fall in showers of flashing pearls, with a shock that shakes the ground. Of course, the various geysers of the Basin are never simultaneously in action. The periods of eruption of all of them are more or less irregular. Many geysers which now exist will, doubtless, sooner or later cease operation, and new ones are forming to take the place of those which dwindle away.

An excellent point from which to obtain a comprehensive view of the Upper Geyser Basin, is a high mound near Old Faithful, formerly the crater of a geyser, of which nothing now is left save a small steaming, gurgling vent. Here the entire band of geysers may be seen and heard as they give their concert with hot water trumpets in perfect diapason, each performer, at irregular intervals, taking a solo part, and uttering his loudest tones in harmonic combination. Close at hand, on the right, is Old Faithful, which regularly, every hour, sends its stream of boiling water 150 feet upward, and continues this spectacle for the space of five long minutes. This grand exhibition is alone sufficient to satisfy the expectations of the most exacting sight-seer. But there are many other geysers, besides, of greater power. In the foreground, looms the Castle, looking like a feudal stronghold, belching forth its pearl-white clouds of steam, and heavy jets of boiling water. To the right, across the river, is the Bee Hive, which, at irregular intervals, sends out a lordly column, 219 feet in height, from its shapely crater. A few rods beyond is the sapphire pool, out of which the Giantess plays, about once a month, her stupendous fountain. Close by are the Lion, the Lioness and her two Cubs, each of which, when roused to action, inspires terror by its growling. Further down the stream, still on the right-hand side, behind an intervening point of pine woods, are the Saw Mill, which keeps up a harsh burring, and the

Grand, which, twice a day, made a display of its majestic power, but is now inactive. Beside these, there are many other geysers of minor calibre, as well as countless steam vents and jets of scalding water, from all of which the flow is carried off by innumerable rills which are stained in brilliant dyes by the mineral deposits. Turning the eye again to the left bank of the Firehole River, and gazing beyond the broad bowl of azure water called the "Beautiful Blue-crested Spring," which almost laves the base of the Castle, a towering column of steam, rushing out of the throat of the Giant like an evil genius ready for mischief, marks the scene of another group of important geysers. The Giant, with high cleft cone, stands close by the river. He is surrounded by a number of noisy retainers, of whom one named Young Faithful is the most vociferous. These all are constantly serving as vents for their brooding master, only ceasing their turbulence, and cowering, as in mute terror, whenever his paroxysms of rage become ungovernable. A short distance to the left of this colossus is the Grotto, whose labyrinths are thickly encrusted with pearls of dazzling lustre. Upon a gentle acclivity, not far to the westward, the Splendid, a young and energetic geyser, improvises a majestic column at least once in three hours, which it decks with luminous vapor like drapery of silver sheen. Then, further on, toward the south, near the extreme end of the Basin, are the Fan, with diverging jets, and the Riverside, rearing itself from the very brink of the stream, each being frequently in action, the last-named shooting a strongly curved column, which breaks into spray and falls into the water like threads of gleaming light, that sparkle and flash with the effulgence of the rainbow, which is visible in the surrounding vapor. There are no less than 440 springs and geysers, according to the report of Dr. Hayden's latest survey, in the Upper Geyser Basin. Of these, at least fifty are known to be really geysers. Among the springs are scores, the

Old Faithful Geyser in Action.

astonishing beauty of which, with respect to the color, depth and translucency of the water, and the wonderful delicacy, variety, and richness of the silicious crystallizations, are not to be described. Geysers exist, it is true, in Iceland and New Zealand; but there are none to be found in groups so magnificent as here, nor are they likely to be reproduced elsewhere on so grand a scale.

In the following more detailed description of the chief geysers and springs of the various basins, the writer has drawn largely for valuable data upon the report recently published by the Department of the Interior of the United States Geological Survey, made under the direction of Dr. F. V. Hayden, in 1878, and especially upon that part of the volume which contains the description, by Dr. A. C. Peale, of the "Thermal Springs of the National Park."

Old Faithful.—This geyser is one of the most interesting in the Park because of the great regularity with which eruptions occur, thus affording excellent opportunities for observation. Its crater, an oblong opening, two by six feet on the inside and four by eight feet on the outside, is situated on a mound of geyserite, measuring at the base 145 by 215 feet, and at the top twenty by fifty-four feet, and rising eleven feet eleven inches above the surrounding level. This mound is composed of layers of deposit in a succession of terraces, which are full of shallow basins. The water in these basins is crystal clear, and the edges of the pools are exquisitely beaded and fretted, their bottoms showing delicate tints of rose, white, saffron, orange, brown and gray. The north end of the crater has large globular masses of beaded pearly deposit, and its throat is of a dark yellow or rusty color. Lieutenant Doane thus describes the deposits around Old Faithful:

"Close around the opening are built up walls eight feet in height, of spherical nodules from six inches to three feet in diameter. These, in turn, are covered on the surface with minute globules of calcareous [silicious] stalagmite [?], encrusted with a thin glazing of silica. The rock at a distance appears the color of ashes of roses, but near at hand shows a metallic gray, with pink and yellow margins of the utmost delicacy. Being constantly wet, the colors are brilliant beyond description. Sloping gently from this rim of the crater in every direction, the rocks are full of cavities, in successive terraces, forming little pools, with margins of silica the color of silver, the cavities being of irregular shape, constantly full of hot water, and precipitating delicate, coral-like beads of a bright saffron. These cavities are also fringed with rock around the edges in meshes as delicate as the finest lace. Diminutive yellow columns rise from their depths, capped with small tablets of rock, and resembling flowers growing in the water. Some of them are filled with oval pebbles of a brilliant white color, and others with a yellowish frost work which builds up gradually in solid stalagmites [?]. Receding still farther from the crater, the cavities become gradually larger and the water cooler, causing changes in the brilliant colorings, and also in the formations of the deposits. * * * The deposits are apparently as delicate as the down on the butterfly's wing, both in texture and coloring, yet are firm and solid beneath the tread. * * * One instinctively touches the hot ledges with his hands, and sounds with a stick the depths of the cavities in the slope, in utter doubt of the evidence of his own eyes."

The eruption of Old Faithful begins with some preliminary splashes or spurts, from three to a dozen or more, which appear like abortive attempts at eruption. These continue for about four minutes, becoming more and more powerful, when they are followed by a rapid succession of jets, which escape with a roar, and soon attain the maximum height. Clouds of steam accompany the water, and reach a much greater height. In a few seconds after the maximum is attained the column dies down, with occasional vigorous spurts. The water eruption is followed by steam, which soon comes out very gently, and finally dies away, leaving the crater empty. The water eruption lasts from four to five minutes, and the steam period is indefinite. The wind causes a great variation in the appear-

General View of Upper Geyser Basin.

ance of the column. The eruption takes place at intervals ranging from fifty-five to seventy minutes, the column of water varying in height from 100 to 150 feet. The temperature of the water in the crater, a few minutes before an eruption, is 200° F., and that of the pools, just after, 170° F. The theoretical boiling point here is 199°, and the temperature above the boiling point is probably caused by the heating of the water during the escape of the superheated steam from far down in the tube of the geyser. Old Faithful is sometimes degraded by being made a laundry. Garments placed in the crater during quiescence are ejected thoroughly washed when the eruption takes place. Gen. Sheridan's men, in 1882, found that linen and cotton fabrics were uninjured by the action of the water, but woolen clothes were torn to shreds.

The Bee Hive.—This geyser is situated about 100 feet from the right bank of the river, near the foot-bridge. It is easily distinguished by its cone, from the resemblance of which to an old-fashioned straw bee hive it was named by the Washburn party in 1870. The crater is three feet in height, and almost circular, measuring three by four feet on top, and having a circumference of twenty feet at the base. It is beautifully coated with beaded silica. There is no surrounding terraced deposit, as there is about most of the craters. This is probably due to the fact that very little water falls around it. The orifice on the summit of the cone measures two feet by three feet, and a line dropped into the tube reaches a depth of twenty-one feet. Just outside of the cone are several vents or steam-holes, one of which acts as a sort of preliminary vent or signal for the eruption of the geyser. The eruption of the Bee Hive is very fine, and peculiar to itself, no other geyser in the basin acting in the same manner. It is preceded by a slight escape of steam, which is soon followed by a column of steam and water, which escapes in a steady stream with great force, much as water is projected from the nozzle of hose used with

Bee Hive Geyser in Action.

steam fire engines. The column is very symmetrical and often exceeds 200 feet in height.

During the latter part of the eruption arrow-shaped jets follow each other to an ex reme height. But little water falls, as the spray is evaporated and carried away as steam.

There is probably little water compared with the amount of steam; but there seems to be a distinct water and steam period. The duration of the former is from three to five minutes, although the spouting is occasionally kept up for fifteen minutes. The force appears to be very great, and the ground is shaken during the action of the geyser. The Bee Hive geyser generally erupts some two to four hours after the Giantess commences, and but rarely independently now. It has, however, been known to go several times in a day without regard to its near rival.

The Giantess —This stupendous geyser is 400 feet from the Bee Hive, on a higher level. It has no raised crater, but disports itself from a large oval aperture thirty-four feet in its greatest length, and twenty-four feet in its widest breadth, on the summit of the mound. It has a broad, gently-sloping mound of deposit about 200 yards in diameter at the base. There is no elevated rim; but the upper layer of the surrounding laminated geyserite projects over the basin, which has a depth of sixty-three feet. It is remarkable for the absence of the handsome ornamentation that is usually seen about the geysers. There is little either in its structure or surroundings to indicate its power. The eruption is not regular, occurring once in about fourteen days, in 1887; but in 1888 its period had lengthened to about four weeks. The pool of this geyser is usually full and boiling gently, giving no warning of an eruption. Cauliflower formations of silicate on the walls of the deep basin are visible to a great depth in the limpid water, which in tint is a sapphire blue. At the time of eruption, the Giantess sends up a grand column, 250 feet into the air, in a series of quick pulsations, which assume the form of separate fountains, one above the other. The eruption of this geyser is accompanied by subterranean tremors and hoarse rumblings which are terrible to feel, especially if one is aroused during the night by the unexpected activity. After the first grand ebullition, the mass of water shot out of the orifice decreases in volume; but the eruption continues with more or less violence at intervals of thirty minutes for twelve or sixteen hours. A chance is thus given to visitors to see this geyser in operation, even though its grandest display take place during the night, when tourists are cozily wrapped in sleep. Mr. N. P. Langford was so fortunate as to see the Giantess in action, and has thus described its appearance:

"No water could be discovered; but we could distinctly hear it gurgling and boiling at a great distance below. Suddenly it began to rise, boiling and spluttering, and sending out huge masses of steam, causing a general stampede of our company, driving us some distance from our point of observation. When within about forty feet of the surface it became stationary, and we returned to look down upon it. It was foaming and surging at a terrible rate, occasionally emitting small jets of hot water nearly to the mouth of the orifice. All at once it seemed seized with a fearful spasm, and rose with incredible rapidity, hardly affording us time to flee to a safe distance, when it burst from the orifice with terrific momentum, rising in a column the full size of this immense aperture to the height of sixty feet; and through and out of the apex of this vast aqueous mass five or six lesser jets or round columns of water, varying in size from six to fifteen inches in diameter, were projected to the marvelous height of 250 feet. These lesser jets, so much higher than the main column and shooting through it, doubtless proceed from auxiliary pipes leading into the principal orifice near the bottom, where the explosive force is greater. * * * This grand eruption continued for twenty minutes, and was the most magnificent sight we ever witnessed. We were standing on the side of the geyser nearest the sun, the gleams of which filled the sparkling columns of water and spray with myriads of rainbows, whose arches were constantly changing,—dipping and fluttering hither and thither, and disappearing only to be succeeded by others, again and again, amid the aqueous column, while the minute globules, into which the spent jets were diffused when falling, sparkled like a shower of diamonds, and around every shadow which the denser clouds of vapor, interrupting the sun's rays, cast upon the column, could be seen a luminous circle, radiant with all the colors of the prism, and resembling the halo of glory represented in paintings as encircling the head of Divinity. All that we had previously witnessed seemed tame in comparison with the perfect grandeur and beauty of this display. Two of these wonderful eruptions occurred during the twenty-two hours we remained in the valley. This geyser we named the Giantess."

Lion, Lioness and Two Cubs.—This group of geysers, sometimes called the "Trinity" and the "Niobe," are situated a short distance west of the Giantess and the Bee Hive, upon a mound, triangular in shape, the summit of which is forty-three feet above the level of the river. The Lioness and Cubs lie close together, and are sometimes in action at the same time, making a beautiful display, although they do not send up a very high column of water. The several craters are highly ornamented with pearl-like beads of geyserite. The Lion, the most powerful of the four geysers, is distant fifty feet from the others, from which it is separated by a slight depression. It has an irregular, flat-topped cone, four feet in height, with an orifice eighteen inches by two and one-half feet, the water in which is always in violent commotion. The outside of the crater is covered with white beaded geyserite, and the throat of the orifice is lined with yellow, pearly-topped, bead-like masses. During eruption the column of water reaches a height of about seventy-five feet.

Saw Mill Geyser.—This is a very active little geyser, on the right side of the river, not far distant from its bank, which attracts attention by its noise. Its eruptions are quite frequent, probably about five or six every twenty-four hours, and continue for a long period. The mass of water ejected is not great; but it is so broken into spray that it presents a beautiful appearance, especially in the bright sunlight, when a rainbow is seen in its fountain-like column. Its basin is shallow, measuring in its outer dimensions forty-three feet in diameter. Inside of this is a second basin, twenty-seven and one-half feet in diameter, covered with pebbles. The outer circle is bordered with spongiform masses, and in the centre the geyser tube is funnel-shaped, seven feet in diameter, sloping to a small orifice. A few feet south of the Saw Mill is the Tardy, a geyser whose action is similar to that of its neighbor, although it spouts less frequently. The Spasmodic and Bulger are minor geysers in the same group.

The Grand Geyser.—In the winter of 1887 and 1888 this magnificent geyser ceased to erupt and is now practically extinct, though the stoppage of the vents of the new spouters near by (the Wave and two smaller geysers) may be followed by a renewal of the eruptions of the Grand. This geyser is situated at the base of a bluff, about 500 feet from the east bank of the river, nearly opposite the Castle Geyser. Unlike many of the principal geysers in the Upper Basin, it has no raised cone, nor even a large, cavernous bowl, to distinguish it. It may be easily recognized, however, by the crater of the Turban, which adjoins it on the north. Its slightly-depressed basin is fifty-two feet in diameter, and only about one foot in greatest depth at the centre. The bottom of the basin is very irregular, and, near the mouth of the geyser tube, it is lined with large, cushion-like masses of geyserite, resembling those of the Turban. In these masses is the orifice, two by four feet in dimensions. There is no raised rim to the basin; but there are shallow pools over the surrounding surface, the irregular formation of which adds to the beauty of the general effect. The Grand usually gave a lordly exhibition at intervals of from sixteen to thirty-one hours. Its action was different from that of the other geysers. There was no particular warning given before an eruption; but the display usually continued with constantly-increasing power about twenty minutes, thus allowing ample time for the visitor to reach the scene during the period of highest activity. The greatest altitude of the column of water is 200 feet; but the steam clouds are vastly higher. During an eruption, a vent thirty feet from the geyser blows off steam with tremendous force. Dr. Peale notes an eruption of the Grand as follows:

"A tremendous rumbling was heard, accompanied by a shaking of the ground, and a huge escape of steam. It would be difficult to describe the feeling of excitement with which we saw the immense column of steam and water shoot from the crater to the height of 200 feet. The column was vertical, and accompanied by immense clouds of steam, and the water in falling shook the ground. It was carried up in a succession of jets, the main mass being large, and the highest jets appearing to be forced through the latter. It was the first geyser of any power that we had seen, and we called it the Grand Geyser. The display lasted altogether about twenty minutes, and, after it was over, the water sank out of sight in the tube."

The Turban Geyser is on the same platform of deposit as the Grand, but three feet higher. It is a small geyser, quite remarkable from the large globular masses in its basin, which resemble the folds of a Turkish head-dress. The water from the Turban splashes over into the basin of the Grand, and often the two geysers are in simultaneous action, although it is not believed that there is any connection between them.

The Castle.—This geyser is the most prominent object, with respect to the size of its cone, in the Upper Basin. It is on the west side of the river, 400 feet from the bank. The crater is situated on the summit of a mound of white and gray deposit which covers about three and one-half acres, and rises forty feet above the level of the river. The Castle well deserves its name; for it strongly resembles the ruin of an ancient stronghold. Its imposing bulk is composed of layer after layer of geyserite, 100 feet in length by 75 feet in width. On the south side, the terraces are much broken, and the cone is greatly marred. The cone is toward the west end of the mound, as viewed from the north, and is twelve feet high, with a circumference at the base of 120 feet. The diameter at the top is twenty feet. The contour is quite irregular, especially on the east side, where there are a series of rough steps of brain-coral formation. This silicious deposit is very firm, and in many places is silvery or leaden gray in color. The orifice of the geyser tube on the summit of the cone is three feet in diameter, nearly circular, and lined with large nodules of a dull orange color. Steam is always escaping from the orifice, and jets of water occasionally spurt above it in the intervals between the eruptions. This geyser usually shoots out a column of water, from thirty to fifty feet in height, once in forty-eight hours, and throws up smaller jets every few minutes. It occasionally, however, husbands its strength for a grand effort, at which times it forces up a beautiful fountain to an altitude of 100 feet or more, accompanied by a tremendous rush of steam. Before each eruption deafening sounds are heard far down the throat of the crater, and masses of water are thrown out. After a short period of quiet, as if gathering force for a new attempt, a fearful roaring, audible for miles distant, takes place, and the ground trembles as from an earthquake. Then, with great violence, the water is ejected to the height before mentioned. There is no doubt that the Castle at one time was the most powerful geyser in the Upper Basin.

One hundred and fifty feet north of the Castle is a large and beautiful boiling spring, known as the "Blue-crested Spring." Its circular basin, measuring a trifle over nineteen feet in diameter, is bordered by a scalloped rim six inches in height, adorned with pearl-like nodules. On the southwest side there is a funnel-shaped crater which measures fourteen by fifteen feet, and the depth of the basin is forty-four feet. The water of this spring is transparent and ethereally blue, and the walls are lined with dazzling white silica. The spring steams gently, and there is, ordinarily, little overflow. But the channel of gray geyserite, which leads from the pool, brightly tinted with yellows and reds, indicates that water is sometimes discharged in great volume. The beauty of this spring can only be appreciated by actual observation. There are scores of others, however, in the Upper Basin, not so large as this, but each possessing features of wonderful attractiveness.

Oblong Geyser.—This is a pool of deep green-blue color, on the river bank, south of the Giant. It is fifty feet in length, and thirty-one feet wide at the end nearest the river. At the bottom are two large bowls of great depth,—the ridge which separates them being seven feet below the surface of the water. The rim of the basin is raised, and elaborately ornamented with large white globular masses. The eruptions, occurring about four times daily, are not very high; but the whole body of water in the basin is tossed upward in a splashing mass, with a great escape of steam, through which occasional jets of water are projected to an altitude of thirty or forty feet. This geyser has sometimes been called the Comet; but the name given it in 1872 is more appropriate.

The Giant.—This geyser is quite near the river, about one-third of a mile below the Castle. It has a cone ten feet in height, which is broken down on one side as if torn away by an eruption of more than ordinary vehemence. The crater is lined with tawny yellow globules of silicate, and is twenty-five feet in depth. The base of the cone measures twenty-four by twenty-five feet, diminishing to eight feet at the top, and the shallow pools of the surrounding platform contain a variety of smooth pebbles of various shapes. This geyser became inactive in the year 1886, but is probably not extinct. It used to erupt every four days, when it played for a period of from one hour and a half to two hours, throwing out a body of water seven feet in diameter, nearly 200 feet high. Those persons who have seen the Giant in operation declare that the volume of water discharged is so great as to double the usual quantity in the river, which, at this point, is seventy-five feet in width. A continuous rumbling is heard during the entire time of the eruption, and the water is steadily held up in a

Giant Geyser in Action.

vertical and majestic column, except when it is swayed by the breeze. There are many vents in the neighborhood of this geyser, which blow off steam and water violently, only ceasing their activity when the Giant himself is aroused. On the same platform with the Giant is another geyser, known as Young Faithful. It has a mound of beautifully beaded geyserite, rising six feet above the level of the terrace. This geyser acts continuously, with irregular spurts from ten to twenty feet.

The Splendid.—This is a very powerful geyser which has developed great energy since 1881. It acts usually at intervals of three hours, sometimes more frequently, throwing out a spreading column of water as high as that of Old Faithful, for a period of five to ten minutes. This geyser is situated on a ridge almost due west from the Giant, and about 200 yards from a conspicuous mound of white geyserite. There would seem to be some confusion as to the name of this geyser, one authority calling it the Comet; but it would seem to be better known by the designation given it by Colonel Norris. There is a smaller geyser, a little to the east, which throws an oblique jet, and sometimes acts simultaneously with the Splendid. The two streams are often connected by a rainbow, which adds to the grandeur of the spectacle. There are many boiling springs of great beauty in this group. One, especially noticeable, is the Punch Bowl, somewhat isolated in its situation, 300 yards southwest of the White Pyramid. It has a crested rim, eighteen inches above the general level, finely beaded, and a large surrounding is formed of silicious deposit.

The Grotto.—This interesting geyser is situated about 200 yards northwest of the Giant. It received its name, says Dr. Peale, from the peculiar shape of the main or larger crater, which is hollowed into fantastic arches, beneath which are grotto-like cavities, that act as lateral orifices for the escape of water during an eruption. The cone, eight feet in height, is very irregular. The orifice is two by six feet, and nineteen feet in depth. On its north side there rises a curious pillar-like mass of geyserite about six feet in height. A second cone is nineteen feet in diameter at the base, and fourteen feet at the top. It is four feet in height, and has a quadrangular orifice measuring three by five feet, in which the water, when not agitated, is from ten to fifteen feet below. The basin is sixteen feet in depth. The entire length of the mound, including the two cones, is fifty-three feet, and the width twenty-six feet; the centres of the two cones being thirty feet apart. The space between them, covered with beaded silica, is raised above the general level, and in it are two small vents that spout during the action of the two large cones. The white and grayish white geyserite, of which the cones and mound are composed, is brittle, and breaks readily into slab-like masses. The eruptions are in two well-defined columns, alternating with each other, with spurts from the small vents. A large portion of the water is thrown into spray, which adds to the effect. The Grotto is in action four times daily, the main column reaching a height of fifty or sixty feet. The interior of the arches and the cavities are lined with a brilliantly white bead-like formation, which glows with the rich opalescent tints that are seen in mother-of-pearl. The Grotto has been aptly termed " the gem of the geysers,— the grotto of pearls."

The Fan and Riverside Geysers.—Crossing again to the east side of the river, two geysers are found. These are the Fan and the Riverside. The former was so named by the party of 1870, because the water during the eruption spreads out in fan-shaped jets, from the fact that there are two craters, the streams from which cross each other. These two craters have orifices of about two feet diameter each, and just below them is a steam-vent called the perpetual spouter, " which sometimes acts in concert with the Fan. The crater of the geyser is composed of pink geyserite, which rises from the river in a series of rounded masses which are beaded with silicate.

The Riverside is 450 feet above, or south of, the Fan, just above the bend of the river. It has a low, irregular mound, with a chimney in the centre. There are two orifices, and it spouts at intervals of about eight hours, the column reaching a height of some ninety to one hundred feet. It is just above the wagon-bridge as the Basin is entered, and unless in action would be given but slight notice as there is little about its crater to attract attention.

Following down the Firehole River a short distance, between the road and the river, is the Morning Glory Spring, the waters of which are of a brilliant blue and its funnel-shaped sides beaded with the most brilliant of formation.

Artemesia Geyser.—Some distance down the river upon the west side of the road is the Artemesia Geyser, situated upon a terrace elevated midway between the level of the river and road. The basin is very large and surrounded by a beautiful formation of pearly geyserite. The sides of the crater may be seen to a great depth when the wind sways the pillar of steam from its surface of crystal water. This geyser was first seen in eruption in 1886. The eruptions are infrequent but very fine, an immense column of water rising some 75 to 100 feet.

The Biscuit Basins.—Quoting from Mr. Walter H. Weed of the U. S. Geological Survey of the Park, who says: " This name is applied to the overflow pools and basins about the Sapphire, the largest spring of the group, because of the resemblance of the deposit in these pools to soda biscuits.

" This group of springs, lying in the flats between the Little Firehole and the Firehole rivers, embraces some of the most beautiful springs of the whole Park. The Sapphire is the largest spring, and like the Artemesia, will perhaps develop into a geyser; but at present the Jewel is the notable geyser, spouting every few minutes to a height of twenty to forty feet, and surrounded by a beautiful deposit, quite unlike anything else in the Upper Geyser Basin. There are also several lesser spouters. The principal springs are named as follows: Shell Basin (a spouter), Mustard (a spouter so named because of its mustard-colored deposit), the Silver Globe, the Sea Weed (which is lined with ropy and leathery forms of algæ), and the Avoca. This last is the most beautiful spring of the group, and shows a beautiful illustration of the formation of silicious sinter (geyserite) by the hot silicious waters. First, by the evaporation of spattered drops. Second, by evaporation at the margin of the pool, producing an extremely thin crust at edge, projecting out over the water. Third, the formation of sinter by the algous jellies, growing in the hot waters. In the gap back of this spring the Little Firehole River leaps over a break in the cliffs of the Madison Plateau and makes the 'Mystic Falls.'"

Lone Star Geyser.—This Geyser is situated in a basin about six miles south from the U. G. B. Hotel, and may only be reached by a trail through a long stretch of down timber. It will, however, repay the tourist for the ride. The cone is some ten feet high, and is finely beaded with pearl-like geyserite, which sparkles in the sunshine with every color. The Lone Star erupts very frequently to a height of fifty or sixty feet, and being little visited, remains the most perfect cone in the Park.

The geysers which have been described are the most important of the Upper Basin, although there are many others of a less striking character. But the fact must be remembered that the periods of activity of all the geysers, with the exception, perhaps, of Old Faithful, vary to some extent from year to year. Absolutely exact statements, therefore, on this point, can not be made. In the main, however, the data given may be depended upon. For the convenience of the reader, the following table of the time of action of the principal geysers in the Upper Basin is presented:

	Name of Geyser.	Interval or Period.	Duration of Eruption.	Height of Column.
1.	Old Faithful	55 to 70 minutes	3 to 5 minutes	100 to 150.
2.	Bee Hive	With Giantess	3 to 18 minutes	170 to 219.
3.	Lioness	Not known	About 3 minutes	60.
4.	Lion	do	About 5 minutes	75.
5.	Giantess	25 to 30 days	12 hours	250.
6.	Saw Mill	Very frequent	1¾ to 3 hours	15 to 20.
7.	Turban	About 15 minutes	15 seco'ds to 5 min.	25.
8.	Castle	Once in 48 hours	30 minutes	100.
9.	Giant	Inactive	1½ hours to 3 hours	130 to over 200.
10.	Young Faithful	Very frequent		10 to 30.
11.	Oblong	Once or twice daily	6 minutes	30 or 40 ft.
12.	Splendid	About 3 hours	4 to 10 minutes	200.
13.	Grotto	Several times a day	Half hour	20 to 60.
14.	Fan	Three times daily	5 to 9 minutes	About 60.
15.	Riverside	Three times daily	10 to 13 minutes	About 100.

Kepler's Cascades.—These beautiful cascades are situated about two miles eastward of Old Faithful Geyser. They consist of a succession of eight or ten cascades of varying height, the highest, perhaps, fifty feet. The water has cut a narrow channel through the basaltic rock, forming a profound cañon through which the torrent frets and fumes in wild tumult. From the best point of observation, a high and rocky plateau some distance below the principal cascade, the scene is quite romantic and picturesque. The foaming waters rush down the gorge, roaring and tumbling against the solid walls of rock which hem them in. The cañon is very deep, and its sheer descent is broken by rough and jagged crags which beetle over the stream. Slender, symmetrical pines, straight as lances, grow on the brink of the cañon, and on the inclosing mountain slopes, as far as the vision reaches. They also cling to every nook and cranny on the sides of the terrible gorge, standing like sentinels on every moss-clad point of vantage. Westward lie the purple mountains, majestic in outline, and clothed with the virgin forest of sombre pine. In the middle distance arise filmy columns of vapor from the geysers and hot springs of the Upper Basin, floating upward and fading into space as an incense offering to the Creator of the wondrously beautiful scene. Kepler's Cascades are really quite bewitching in their loveliness, the harmony of the picture leaving nothing to be desired, as the romantic is here picturesquely perfect, the colors of the vegetation on the rocks in contrast to the foaming water delighting the eye. The visitor reluctantly leaves this idyllic spot.

Shoshone Lake.—This beautiful sheet of water, situated about nine miles south of the Upper Geyser Basin, from which there is a good trail leading to it, is almost in the shape of a purse, its outlet being at the bottom of the larger lobe, by a broad and sluggish stream, three miles in length, connecting it with Lewis Lake. Its greatest length is six miles and a

Kepler's Cascades, on the Firehole River.

half, and its greatest width four miles and a half, while the stricture is only half a mile across, and the total area of the lake is not over twelve square miles. The shores are almost everywhere bold and densely covered with timber. On its southwestern arm is an interesting geyser basin, of which the Union Geyser is the principal attraction. This geyser has three small mounds or craters close together, each of which has an opening or vent. The three spout simultaneously, although the smallest one is rather insignificant. During eruption a column of water over one hundred feet in height, with volumes of steam, is projected with a steady roar and great force. The bead-like geyserite formation about these craters is quite beautiful, the color grading from yellow into gray, with pearly tints. Another geyser in this basin, called the "Minute Man," has also a very finely ornamented crater, while the Shield, the Gourd, the Little Bulger and the Little Giant are also minor geysers well worthy of inspection. There are many boiling springs in the basin of wonderful beauty.

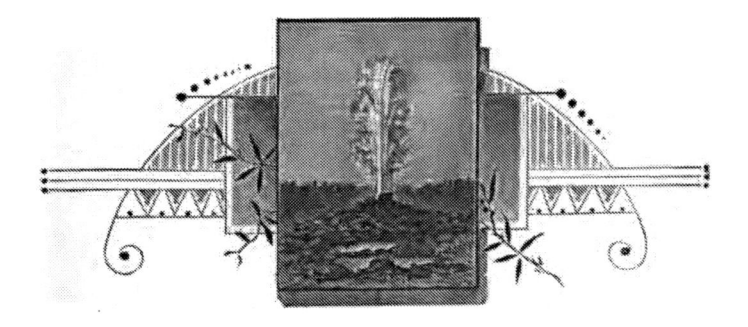

THE RETURN TRIP.

The tourist may return by either of the roads to the Lower Geyser Basin. And by fortune's favor may be amply repaid by the chance of once more witnessing the Excelsior Geyser in action. Should he be so fortunate, his second impression will probably be a much-added-to appreciation of the grandeur of this majestic geyser, especially if he witnessed the former eruption from a near point of view. With many, the first impression is one of awe and terror at the geyser's violence. A broad and level highway, shaded much of the way by stately pine, leads up the west side of the river, and brings one, by a short drive, to the Firehole Hotel.

From here, by a so far untraveled road, we follow down the main river a distance, and then seeking the foot-hills of the ridge we gradually ascend only to drop rapidly down to Cañon Creek on the other slope. From this crossing the tourist may take a fifteen-minute walk, and by following down Cañon Creek and up the Gibbon River, gain with ease the best possible view of the Gibbon Falls. Usually, however, the road is followed up the divide, and the tourist gains his view of the falls from the cañon directly above them.

Falls of the Gibbon.—These are situated four miles from the entrance to the cañon. The water tumbles over the precipice in a foamy sheet, eighty feet in height, making a charming picture, full of life and vigor, which is in striking contrast to its setting of grim rocks and dusky pines.

The Gibbon Canon.—The towering walls of the Gibbon Cañon, at one place 2,000 feet in height, completely overshadow the road, and present a perfect picture of a wild and romantic mountain gorge. The river is bordered by many small geysers and boiling springs, which impress their strangeness and beauties upon the mind, and any one of which would draw multitudes to see it, and to marvel at it, if only it stood apart from this lavish exhibit of wonderful things.

Falls of the Gibbon River.

Monument Geyser Basin.—Just at the entrance of the Gibbon Cañon, to the left of the road, there is a foot-bridge over the stream. This leads to a trail on the opposite bank, pursuing which about a mile and a half over the rough slope of Mount Schurz, and at an elevation of 1,000 feet above the river, the "Monument Geyser Basin" is reached. This trip may be made in the saddle, although great caution must be exercised in fording the stream, lest the horse's feet be scalded in the boiling springs which line the banks. The Basin, five acres in extent, is the scene of a body of nearly extinct geysers and hissing springs. The grotesque shapes of the geyser cones and their monumental appearance give the name of the Basin its significance. There are twelve of these monumental cones, ranging in height from six to twenty feet, all of which have orifices in the top. From a few of these fumaroles volumes of steam constantly issue; the majority, however, are apparently lifeless, and are fast crumbling away. One of these cones somewhat resembles a crouching lioness; another, a headless man; a third, like a slender chimney, pours out a cloud of smoke; a fourth whistles like a locomotive; a fifth belches out steam with a whizzing sound which is quite deafening as you stand by, and is audible for miles. A stout pine limb placed over its vent will, in about a minute, dry and shrivel in the superheated steam and drop asunder. There are also caldrons of boiling sulphur and drab-colored mud, besides numerous frying-pans and puffing holes. Around the rims of the pools are beautiful crystals of sulphur, like frost and bead work. This Basin is only a dwindling fragment of what it was at no remote period; but its curious features are, nevertheless, well worth looking at. The view of Elk Park and the river from the crest of the mountain spur is also quite enjoyable.

Once more following the road northward, we leave the Gibbon River Cañon, and cross Elk Park, a meadow about five miles in circumference. Some three miles beyond the meadow's extremity is the Norris Geyser Basin. Just as we enter Elk Park, however, is another point well worth the time necessary for a visit.

The Gibbon Paint Pot Basin.—This wonderful area, several acres in extent, is situated in the woods to the right of the road, about half a mile eastward of the bluff at the head of the Gibbon Cañon. Clouds of vapor sufficiently indicate the locality. There are, perhaps, five hundred mud and boiling springs in the Basin. They are not in groups, but interspersed with Nature's charming fickleness. It is one of the most curious sights to watch the great pots of gurgling, splashing and exploding mud. Every color and shade of color is represented,—white, orange, green, violet, purple, blue, brown and drab. Clots of this pasty material, smooth to the touch as velvet, are constantly thrown out and banked up around the craters. The noise made by the bubbling compound is not unlike the thud of a steamer's paddles striking the water. The hot springs are of divers colors, and the water invariably as limpid as crystal. Some of the pools are as green as an emerald, others as blue as a turquoise, and one spouting fountain is red as blood. Indeed, the delicacy and variety of the coloring and the beauty of the formations within the springs and on their scalloped margins are bewildering in their opulence. The water is highly impregnated with various salts, and the vapor reeks strongly. The many-tinted earths which are heaped around the paint pots appear like the purest porcelain mass, ready for moulding by the potter. Over all the operations in this strange natural laboratory there is a pall of vapor which issues from clefts in the ground and fissures on the sides of the sombre, tree-clad hills.

The homeward trip is then resumed, and reaching the Norris Geyser Basin, we retrace our road from there past Beaver Lake, Obsidian Cliffs, and passing down through Kingman's Pass on the Golden Gate road, the starting point, Mammoth Hot Springs, is reached.

Monument Geysers, and Gibbon Basin Paint Pots.

MOUNT WASHBURN AND TOWER FALLS.

From the Mammoth Hot Springs to Yancey's, for twenty miles there is an excellent wagon-road. Several miles of good trail bring the tourist to Tower Falls. The country traversed is wonderfully diversified. For a short space the valley of the main Gardiner is followed. Then the road leads by the grand cañon of the East Gardiner, affording an opportunity to see the very beautiful falls of this stream, situated something over four miles from the starting point. Leaving the East Fork to the right hand, the road passes over the grassy plateaus and lava beds of the valleys of Black-tail Deer and other creeks, beside the yawning fissures fronting Hell-roaring Creek, through the wild gorge known as Dry Cañon, and down the mountain slopes 2,000 feet to Pleasant Valley and Baronette's Bridge at the Forks of the Yellowstone River. This bridge is over the main stream, not far from its confluence with the East Fork. It was constructed for the benefit of the miners at Cooke City, on the Clark's Fork, about fifty miles distant, in the Big Horn Mountains. Its proprietor, Jack Baronette, is one of the most famous guides and hunters in the country. Leaving the bridge, the trail follows the west side of the Yellowstone, at first quite near the stream, but gradually bearing to the west until Tower Creek is reached.

Tower Falls.—About three miles south of this bridge, Tower Creek, which is a rapid, snow-fed brook, twelve or fifteen feet wide and one or two feet deep, joins the Yellowstone. The creek flows for about ten miles through a narrow, rugged, and precipitous cañon, enclosed by walls 300 to 400 feet high. Two hundred yards above its entrance into the

Tower Falls, From Above.

Yellowstone the stream pours over an abrupt descent of 132 feet into a deep, gloomy gorge, so narrow that the sun's rays scarcely penetrate it. The Falls are not unlike those of "Minnehaha," inasmuch as there is a clear, safe passage between them and the wall behind them; but they have eight or ten times the mass of water, and are three or four times as high. These falls are surrounded by columns of volcanic breccia, rising fifty feet above them, standing like the towers upon some mediæval fortress. Describing these columns, Mr. N. P. Langford, first Superintendent of the Park, said:

"Some resemble towers, others the spires of churches, and others still shoot up little and slender as the minarets of a mosque. Some of the loftiest of these formations, standing upon the very brink of the Falls, are accessible to an expert and adventurous climber. The position attained on one of these narrow summits, amid the uproar of waters, at the height of 200 feet above the boiling chasm, as the writer can affirm, requires a steady head and strong nerves, yet the view which rewards the temerity of the exploit is full of compensations. Below the fall the stream descends in numerous rapids with frightful velocity through a gloomy gorge to its union with the Yellowstone. Its bed is filled with enormous boulders, against which the rushing waters break with great fury. Many of the capricious formations wrought from the shale excite merriment as well as wonder. Of this kind especially is the huge mass, sixty feet in height, which, from its supposed resemblance to the proverbial foot of his Satanic Majesty, is called the Devil's Hoof. The scenery of mountain, rock and forest surrounding the falls, is very beautiful. The name of Tower Falls was, of course, suggested by some of the most conspicuous features of the scenery."

The following is an extract from the report of Lieut. Doane, U. S. A., who escorted Mr. Langford's party:

"The sides of the chasm are worn into caverns lined with various tinted mosses nourished by clouds of spray which rise from the cataract; while above and to the left a spur from the great plateau rises over all with a perpendicular front of 400 feet. Nothing can be more chastely beautiful than this lovely cascade, hidden away in the dim light of overshadowing rocks and woods, its very voice hushed to a low murmur, unheard at the distance of a few hundred yards. Thousands might pass within a half-mile, and not dream of its existence; but once seen, it passes to the list of most pleasant memories."

An excellent view of these falls may be had by ascending the cliff above them. But by far the best and most satisfactory prospect is obtained by walking down to the mouth of Tower Creek, and following the stream upward through the majestic gateway to the foot of the cataract.

The bridle-road to Mount Washburn crosses Tower Creek just above the Falls. Then it ascends, by a very easy grade, the long spur which separates Antelope from Tower Creek. Passing the shoulder of the spur, where it turns to the southward, the trail begins a general descent toward the gorge of Carnelian Creek. For several miles it continues this course on the side of the mountain, crossing the sharp gulches of two or three mountain torrents, and finally reaches the bed of the cañon a short distance below the head of the creek. Then it goes up a steep ascent to the divide, which has an elevation of 8,867 feet. On the summit is a spring, the water from which drains either way. Mount Washburn may be ascended to its very summit on horseback without greatly distressing the animals. South of the Washburn Divide, the trail skirts the base of the mountains westward, gradually descending to the valley of Cascade Creek. It then follows this valley down to the neighborhood of the Falls of the Yellowstone, crossing Cascade Creek just above Crystal Falls.

Another, and in some respects a better, bridle path from Tower Falls to the Falls of the Yellowstone than that described, has been recently opened. This route avoids several steep ascents, ascending by easy grades the upland meadows of Antelope Creek to the summit of Rowland's Pass to Mount

Washburn, thence descending this elevation by a moderate dip to the brink of the Grand Cañon. An accessible peak, about half a mile east of Rowland's Pass, near the verge of the Grand Cañon, affords a commanding view of the entire length of the latter, in all its windings from the Forks to the Great Falls. By a short and not difficult ascent, west from the summit of the Pass, an open spur is reached, which in less than two miles of gradual upward travel, leads to the highest point of Mount Washburn. This new road then skirts the eastern base of Mount Washburn, crossing Glade Creek, passing by a group of hot springs, and, a mile and a half beyond, strikes Meadow Camp and the forks of the Painted Cliff trail, below the Great Falls.

View from Mount Washburn.—The Rev. Wayland Hoyt, D. D., of Brooklyn, who visited the Park in 1878, thus gives his impression of the view from Mount Washburn:

"Let us take our stand for a little now upon Mount Washburn. Its rounded crest is more than 10,000 feet above the level of the sea, and perhaps 5,000 feet above the level of the valley out of which it springs. Its smooth slopes are easy of ascent. You need not dismount from your horse to gain its summit. Standing there, you look down upon the whole grand panorama as does that eagle yonder, holding himself aloft upon almost motionless wings. I doubt if there is another view at once so majestic and so beautiful in the whole world. Your vision darts through the spaces for 150 miles on some sides. You are standing upon a mountain lifting itself out of a vast saucer-shaped depression. Away yonder, where the sky seems to meet the earth on every side around the whole circumference of your sight, are lines and ranges of snow-capped peaks shutting your glances in. Yonder shoots upward the serrated peak of Pilot Mountain, in the Clark's Fork Range. Joined to that, sweep on around you in the dim distance the snowy lines of the Madison Range. Yonder join hands with these the Stinking Water Mountains, and so on and on and around. Do you see that sharp pinnacle-pointed mountain away off at the southwest, shining in its garments of white against the blue of the summer sky? That is Mount Evarts, named after the poor lost wanderer who for thirty-seven days of deadly peril and starvation sought a way of escape from these frowning mountain barriers which shut him in so remorselessly, and it marks the divide of the Continent.

"Take now a closer view for a moment. Mark the lower hills folded in their thick draperies of pine and spruce, like dark green velvet of the softest and the deepest; notice, too, those beautiful park-like spaces where the trees refuse to grow, and where the prairie spreads its smooth sward freely toward the sunlight. And those spots of steam breaking into the vision every now and then, and floating off like the whitest clouds that ever graced the summer sky,—those are the signals of the geysers at their strange duty, yonder in the geyser basins, thirty miles away. And those bits of silver flashing hither and thither on the hillsides amid the dense green of the forests,—these are water-falls and fragments of ice glaciers, which for ages have been at their duty of sculpturing these mountains, and have not yet completed it. And that lovely deep blue sheet of water, of such a dainty shape, running its arms out toward the hills, and bearing on its serene bosom emeralds of islands,—that is the sweetest sheet of water in the world,—that is the Yellowstone Lake. And that exquisite broad sheen of silver, winding through the green of the trees and the brown of the prairie,—that is the Yellowstone River, starting on its wonderful journey to the Missouri, and thence downward to the Gulf, between 6,000 and 7,000 miles away. But, nearer to us, almost at our feet, as we trace this broad line of silver, the eye encounters a frightful chasm, as if the earth had suddenly sunk away; and into its gloomy depths the brightness and beauty of the shining river leaps, and is thenceforward lost altogether to the view. That is the tremendous cañon or gorge of the Yellowstone."

FOSSIL FORESTS AND HOODOO REGION.

Although the Grand Tour, with such extra excursions as have been noted, covers the roads, bridle-paths and trails which are used by the great majority of visitors, it by no means exhausts the possibilities of travel within the Park limits. The road from Baronette's Bridge to the Clark's Fork Mines, for example, leads through magnificent mountain scenery, and also traverses one of the principal fossil forest regions in the Park. The bridle-path, leaving this road near Soda Butte Springs, and following the south bank of the East Fork, conducts, twenty-nine miles from Soda Butte and about forty-five miles from Baronette's Bridge, to the Hoodoo or Goblin Mountains, without a brief description of whose wonders this little volume would be incomplete.

Petrified Forests.—The basins of the East Fork of the Yellowstone, and of Pelican, Tower and Black Tail Creeks, constitute an area of petrified forest growths on a scale hitherto unknown. One of the most easily accessible of the fossilized forest areas is situated to the southwest of Pleasant Valley, about four miles from Baronette's Bridge. There are not so many petrified tree trunks standing here as are to be seen at some other points; but the tourist will, nevertheless, be fully repaid by turning off from the road and examining these curious objects. On the south side of the Third Cañon, also, nearly opposite Hell-roaring Creek, is a massive promontory, composed of conglomerates, in which are numerous beds of sandstones and shales. The greater part of these strata is filled with the silicified remains of successive forest growths, which often appear in relief upon the face of the height, the trees sometimes standing upright just as they grew, rising in vertical layers one above the other, with the roots of each succeeding forest showing above the tops of the previous one. On the north face of Amethyst Mountain, which is on the East Fork of the Yellowstone River, is a section of these strata, upward of 2,000 feet in height. The bed of the river is at an elevation of 6,700 feet above the sea, and the summit of Amethyst Mountain 9,423. The view from this peak is wonderfully grand. Specimens found in the mountain are mainly impure amethysts and forms of quartz chalcedony. Here the ground is strewn with trunks and limbs of trees which have been petrified into solid, clear white agate. In the steeper middle portion of the mountain's face, rows of upright trunks stand out on the ledges like the columns of a ruined temple. Farther down the slope the petrified tree trunks fairly cover the surface, and were at first supposed to be the shattered remains of a recent forest. Prostrate trunks fifty and sixty feet in length are of frequent occurrence, not a few of them being as much as five or six feet in diameter. The strata which inclose these trunks are composed chiefly of fine-grained greenish sandstones, indurated clays, and moderately coarse conglomerates. These strata contain many animal and vegetable remains; snakes, toads and fishes, branches, rootlets and fruits. Digging down among the petrified roots, are to be found large clusters of the most beautiful crystallizations of all shades, from delicate pink to deep cherry. In most cases the woody structure of the trees is well preserved, and, where the trunks have broken into sections, on the exposed ends the lines of growth, from centre to circumference, can be counted with ease. In many cases the wood is completely opalized or agatized, and such cavities as exist in the decayed trunks are filled with beautiful crystals of quartz and calcite. Nearly all the crystals that occur so plentifully in this region have been formed in the hollows of silicified trees.

Hoodoo Region, or Goblin Land.—The Hoodoo Region

is the mountaineer term for the eroded portion of the Sierra Shoshone Mountains, which lies outside the eastern boundary of the Park, between the Passamaria or Stinking-water Fork of the Big Horn, and the head branches of the East Fork of the Yellowstone River. This strange locality is situated about forty-five miles southeast of Baronette's Bridge. It was discovered in 1870 by a party of miners prospecting for gold, and has been visited thus far by only a few tourists. Colonel Norris reached this region by ascending the valley of the East Fork of the Yellowstone in 1880, having been driven back by Indians two years before while endeavoring to explore in this direction. These Indians were encamped upon an elevated plateau, screened by firs, commanding a fine view of all the approaches. In 1880, when this old camp was visited, there was abundant evidence that it had been frequently occupied by the red men during the summer season after border raids and massacres, the ground being strewn with remnants of clothing, blankets and china-ware. The Hoodoo region is high up the mountain, and the trail leading to it is over a wild and rough country, the difficulties of which only the most enterprising tourists are willing to encounter. The Hoodoo or Goblin Mountain, is 10,700 feet in height, and about one mile in length. Glacial action has worn an extensive labyrinth in the conglomerate breccia and the volcanic rocks. Upon the southern face of the mountain, extending from 500 to 1,500 feet below the summit, the frosts and storms of ages have worn numberless deep, narrow, crooked channels amid the slender tottering pillars, shafts, mounds and pyramids which form this singular maze. The formations are totally unlike in shape those seen in other eroded districts. They are not symmetrical, but assume every curious and fantastic form, among which may be seen gigantic figures of beasts, birds and reptiles. One mound is described as looking like a large altar pyre, 125 feet in height, resting on a pyramidal base, the sacrificial victim lying on the top. Two monumental blocks, thirty feet in height, appear to be surmounted by great recumbent birds. Some of the enormous columns take the shape of petrified bears sitting upon their haunches. One tall pillar, almost a perfect obelisk in form, resting upon a massive rectangular pedestal, has a large sandstone boulder adhering to its side, about one-third distant from its base, as if fixed there by magnetic attraction. There is a cone-shaped monument, 100 feet high, which poises most deftly upon one of two slender points at its apex an immense boulder. Near by is a bulky, dome-like formation, which supports upon its summit what appears to be a mammoth mushroom. Indeed, there is no end to the strange and spectral shapes which are met in these weird labyrinths at every turn. The rocks are of all shades of color, and, in many places, among the winding passages between them, are tunnels in the ice and snow which afford safe hiding places for the mountain sheep. Mysterious undulating sounds, heard *overhead* in this region, only serve to intensify the by no means agreeable feeling excited in the traveler by its weird and preternatural appearance. According to Colonel Norris, eagles hover in large numbers over the Hoodoo Mountain, finding subsistence upon the carcasses of the lambs which they make their prey, by hurling the animals from the crags upon the jagged rocks hundreds of feet below. Sometimes the feasts of these crafty birds are terminated by the appearance of the cougar or the sneaking wolverine upon the scene.

During the summer of 1888, Mr. W. H. Weed, of the United States Geological Survey, discovered a new point of interest on Cache Creek, a mile above the trail leading into the Hoodoo Basin. The place has been named Death Gulch. It is a narrow ravine running up the mountain from the Cache Creek some 250 feet, and ending, or rather beginning, in a "scoop" or basin. In this scoop or ravine were found the remains of five bear, an elk, and numerous small animals. The strong smell of sulphur, and a choking sensation of the lungs, indicated the presence of noxious gases, which had certainly asphyxiated many victims; for of these remains one silver-tip grizzly was perfectly fresh. And it seems probable that the floods of early spring wash everything from the gulch each season.

FAUNA OF THE PARK.

Wild animals exist in large numbers and in great variety. The killing of any kind of game is, however, prohibited, and a heavy fine and imprisonment are the penalty attached to any violation of this ordinance. The Park is admirably suited to the purpose of preserving many species of the fauna of the United States from extinction, which, without protection, are certain at no distant day to disappear before the advance of settlement and civilization. The elevated plateau which is inclosed by the mountain chain, extending from the southeastern arm of the Yellowstone Lake to Slough Creek and Tower Creek, affords a fine pasture ground for bison, elk, bighorn, moose, and other noble game. Here, at least, in the interest of natural history, specimens of our largest game animals should be carefully preserved. Bison, differing in many features from the buffalo of the plains, roam in scattered bands in the valleys of the Crevice, Hell-roaring and Slough Creeks, and also on the elevation extending from the Hoodoo region to the Grand Cañon, and from Amethyst Mountain to Pelican Creek, near the foot of Yellowstone Lake. They also pasture upon the Madison Plateau and Little Madison River. Elk are found all through the Park, and more especially in the numerous grassy openings on the mountain sides, which are admirably adapted for their haunts. Herds of two and three hundred are often seen at a time. Between the Mammoth Hot Springs and Cooke City, near the northeast corner of the Park, just outside the limits, there are said to be at least 5,000 elk, of which the yearly increase, at a very low estimate, may be placed at 1,000. Moose are sometimes seen near the Lake of the Woods, but generally rove in heavily timbered and marshy regions. Their main haunts are in the thickly wooded and swampy places around the fingers and thumb of the Yellowstone Lake, and in the willow and beaver swamps. They keep also in the boggy inlets of Shoshone, Lewis and Heart Lakes, and the Snake River region, to the Tetons. Black-tail and white-tail deer feed in the densely timbered valleys and foot-hills, and also along the creeks. Antelope, though not numerous, still make their haunts in the valleys of the Upper Gardiner River, and up the East Fork to Soda Butte, and in the Madison Valley. They frequent many of the creeks, but keep mainly in the open regions. Big-horn sheep are in abundance all through the Park. They choose the mountain crests as well as the craggy spurs, and are also found near the foot-hills. Within the limits of the Park, but usually confined to the main range of the Rocky Mountains, are various species of the bear tribe. Wolverine, or long-tailed mud-bear, frequent the foot-hills, and the densely timbered spots in the valleys, ready to steal and carry away what the bear, wolf or lion slaughters. Wolves have become quite scarce. They still, however, rove in many portions of the Park. Foxes, red, gray, and black, are numerous. There are also to be found coyotes, badgers, otters, beavers, minks, martens, sables, ermines, rabbits, hares, moles, mice, rats, muskrats, porcupines, rock dogs, squirrels, chipmunks and skunks. There are numbers of birds, comprising many varieties of ducks, grouse, owls and hawks; several varieties of eagles and vultures; also cranes, blackbirds, jackdaws and bluejays, geese, brant, pelicans, swans, crows and ravens. The waters of the Park are well stocked with trout and grayling of excellent quality, except in the Yellowstone Lake, where the trout are infested with worms. No reason can be given for this peculiarity in this special locality, for everywhere else the fish are very fine. There seem to be but few reptiles in the Park. The rattlesnake has been found only in the Yellowstone Valley below the Mammoth Hot Springs.

FLORA OF THE PARK.

Of the area of the Park—3,575 square miles—no less than 2,751 square miles, seventy-seven per cent., are covered with dense forests. The principal varieties are the black or bastard fir, black spruce, white pine, red fir and balsam fir. The black fir is the most plentiful, often growing from three to five feet in diameter and 150 feet in height. It is usually found on elevated terraces and near the Mammoth Hot Springs, Tower Falls and the Upper Yellowstone. Black spruce equals the black fir in height, though not in diameter. It is much more majestic, and is preferable for lumbering purposes. It grows on sheltered slopes of the mountains and in moist places. White pine is marked for its symmetrical beauty, and is generally found in valleys, near creeks and cañon passes of the mountains. It grows very dense, rendering traveling among it difficult and fatiguing, and proving a great impediment in exploring and cutting bridle-paths and roads. Red fir is abundant throughout the Park, and comes first in value, standing unrivaled as timber for building culverts, bridges, terraces, etc. Balsam fir is also plentifully found within this region, growing in beautiful groves, or scattered here and there over grassy slopes, and dotting the foot-hills of the mountains. Of the smaller kinds of trees, there are an abundance of red or spotted cedar, poplar or aspen, dwarf maple and innumerable dense thickets of willow. It is very much to be regretted that immense tracts of woodland have been burned over. As a consequence it is not uncommon, in going through the Park, to be compelled to pass by mile after mile of charred and blackened tree trunks, instead of riding in the refreshing shade of the woods. In addition to the forest growths, there are many kinds of shrubs, flowers and grasses. The choke cherry, the gooseberry, the buffalo-berry, the bull-berry, and black and red currants are found along the streams and in moist places of the middle and lower altitudes. The meadows and hillsides are spangled with bright-colored flowers, among which may be noted the bee-larkspur, the columbine, the harebell, the lupin, the evening primrose, the aster, the painted cup, the gentian, and various kinds of euphorbia. It is not uncommon to find daisies, buttercups, forget-me-nots, white ground phlox and other field flowers flourishing in profusion near the melting snow banks during the month of August. A lady who crossed Mount Washburn, in the summer of 1885, gathered no fewer than fifty-two varieties of flowers on the heights of that mountain. Scarcely a night throughout the year passes without frost, even though the temperature by day is over 80° F., so that all forms of vegetation in the Park grow and bloom under somewhat unusual conditions. Indeed, when ice forms during the night, as often happens, and the petals of the flowers become crisp with frost, even then the blooms are not harmed, but thaw out bright and fresh when the hot sun touches them. The pasturage on the many open spaces is excellent, the mountain meadows being covered with a mat of nutritious grasses. The predominating variety is the bunch grass, upon which horses subsist without the need of oats. Among the other kinds are the blue-joint, fescue and beard grasses, as well as Alpine timothy, all of which grow luxuriantly.

APPENDIX.

Distances in National Park.—The following are the distances between various points of interest embraced in the grand tour:

	MILES.	Continuous trip. MILES.
Mammoth Hot Springs to		
Falls of the West Gardiner (Golden Gate)	4	4
Crossing of Middle Fork of Gardiner River	3	7
Willow Park (upper end)	3	10
Obsidian Cliffs, Beaver Lake	2	12
Norris Geyser Basin	7	19
Head of Gibbon Canon (about)	5	24
Falls of the Gibbon River	4	28
Forks of the Firehole River (Lower Geyser Basin)	8	36
Excelsior Geyser (in midway Geyser Basin)	4	40
Old Faithful (in Upper Geyser Basin)	5½	45½

ROAD ON EAST SIDE OF RIVER.

Forks of the Firehole River to Fountain Geyser	3		
Excelsior Geyser	2	5	
Old Faithful	5½	10½	
Returning			56
Lower Geyser Basin to Junction of roads (return) leading to Yellowstone Lake and Great Falls			81
Sulphur Mountain	2	27	83
Upper Falls of the Yellowstone	5	32	88
Great Falls of the Yellowstone	1	33	89
Lookout Point	1	34	90
Inspiration Point	1	35	91
Great Falls to Norris Geyser Basin by Virginia Cañon road	11	0	102
Mammoth Hot Springs	19	0	121
Old Faithful to Kepler's Cascades			2
Old Faithful to Shoshone Lake and Geyser Basin			12
Forks of road to Mud Geyser (Yellowstone Lake road)			2
Yellowstone Lake	6		8
Great Falls to Mt. Washburn	9		
Tower Falls	6		15
Yancey's	3		18
Black-tail Deer Creek	11		29
East Fork Gardiner River	4		33
Mammoth Hot Springs	2		35
Yancey's to Soda Butte	16		
Goblin Mountain in Hoodoo Region	29		45
Lower Geyser Basin on Madison Cañon road to west boundary of Park	14		

Elevations in National Park.—From the reports of the Geological Survey made under the direction of Dr. F. V. Hayden in 1878, the following table of altitudes, giving the more important points within the limits of the National Park, is taken :

	FEET.
Amethyst Mountain	9,423
Bunsen's Peak	8,775
Cascade Creek	7,912
Crater Hills, or Sulphur Mountain	7,820
Divide between Yellowstone and Madison Rivers	8,164
Dunraven Peak	9,988
Gardiner River, mouth of	5,300
Gibbon River, head of cañon	7,350
Lower Geyser Basin	7,252
Madison Lake	8,300
Madison River, at foot of second cañon	6,605
Mammoth Hot Springs.	
At Hotel	6,387
Summit above on Norris Road	7,310
Mary's Lake	8,336
Mount Doane	10,713
Mount Evarts	7,600
Mount Langford	10,799
Mount Stevenson	10,420
Mount Washburn	10,346
Mud Geysers on Yellowstone River	7,712
Norris Geyser Basin	7,527
Quadrant Mountain	10,127
Shoshone Geyser Basin	7,881
Shoshone Lake	7,830
Upper Geyser Basin, near Old Faithful	7,372
Yellowstone Lake	7,738
Yellowstone River :	
At Mud Geysers	7,705
Upper Fall, top	7,693
Upper Fall, bottom	7,581
Lower Fall, top	7,575
Lower Fall, bottom	7,275
Mouth Tower Creek	6,207
Mouth East Fork	5,970
Yellowstone Cañon, east side, top of, at falls	7,710

APPENDIX.

The Climate.—Meteorological observations taken in the Park do not extend over a long series of years. But enough is known of the climate to warrant the assertion that July, August and September are the very best months for tourists. There are no really intensely hot summer days, and visitors should always wear woolen underclothing. After sunset, even on the very warmest days in August, the air becomes delightfully cool, and two or three heavy blankets as bed covering are never unwelcome. Indeed, a night without frost is the exception. The snow lies a long time; but, even in the depths of winter, the Park is not a very cold place. From reports made by Col. Norris, during a period of three years, the following summary of the weather at the Mammoth Hot Springs, during the ordinary tourist season, is given:

FOR JULY.

1879. Sunrise, 59°; midday, 80°; sunset, 63°; mean, 67°.
1880. Sunrise, 50°; midday, 68°; sunset, 62°; mean, 60°.
1881. Sunrise, 55°; midday, 77°; sunset, 69°; mean, 67°.

FOR AUGUST.

1879. Sunrise, 49°; midday, 74°; sunset, 69°; mean, 64°.
1880. Sunrise, 50°; midday, 68°; sunset, 64°; mean, 61°.
1881. Sunrise, 50°; midday, 79°; sunset, 66°; mean, 65°.

FOR SEPTEMBER.

1879. Sunrise, 39°; midday, 60°; sunset, 53°; mean, 51°.
1880. Sunrise, 41°; midday, 66°; sunset, 53°; mean, 55°.
1881. Sunrise, 36°; midday, 61°; sunset, 50°; mean, 46°.

FOR OCTOBER.

1879. Sunrise, 41°; midday, 57°; sunset, 52°; mean, 50°.
1880. Sunrise, 32°; midday, 57°; sunset, 42°; mean, 44°.
1881. Sunrise, 29°; midday, 49°; sunset, 39°; mean, 39°.

Temperature of the Geysers and Hot Springs.—There is a wide range of difference in the temperature of the water of the several geysers and groups of springs. Repeated tests have shown that there is even a variation of a few degrees in the temperature of the same geyser at different periods. This is doubtless due to degrees of intensity in activity. It is not believed that the temperature of the air has any appreciable effect upon the temperature of the water, except, perhaps, upon the surface of the largest pools. The boiling point at the altitude of the principal geyser and hot spring basins is from thirteen to fifteen degrees Fahrenheit lower than at the sea level (212° F.). Consequently, the water of many geysers and springs is boiling even though it may mark only 197° F. of heat. The water of Old Faithful and the Bee Hive, in the Upper Basin, as well as that of some other geysers and springs in other portions of the Park, often marks 200° F. at the surface, and this temperature is rarely exceeded. The Saw Mill water is usually about 185° F., that of the Grand, 189°; the Turban, 195°; the Castle, 193°; the Giant, 194°; the Grotto, 198°; the Giantess and the Lion, each 199°; and the Lioness, 188°. The taste of geyser and hot-spring water is decidedly disagreeable to most people, especially when it is taken quite hot; but it would seem to be not at all unwholesome.

Bunsen's Theory of Geyser Formation and Action.—According to Bunsen and other geological authorities, a geyser does not find a cave or even a perpendicular tube ready made out of which to flow, but, like a volcano, forms its own crater. If the water be not alkaline, the spring will remain an ordinary boiling spring. But if alkaline, the water will hold silica in solution, and the silica will be deposited about the spring. Thus a mound and tube are gradually built. For a long time, a spring of this character may boil, but not be violently eruptive, the circulation maintaining nearly an equal temperature in every part of the tube. But, as the tube becomes longer, and the circulation more and more impeded, the difference of temperature in the water in the upper and lower parts of the tube grows greater and greater, until, at length, the boiling point is reached below, while the water above is comparatively cool. Then begins the eruption, to be repeated with more or less frequency for a period of years. Finally, either from the gradual failure of the subterranean heat, or else from the increasing length of the tube, by which the formation of steam is repressed, the eruptions gradually cease. Bunsen notes geysers in every stage of development, some being playful springs without tubes; others not yet eruptive, having short tubes; still others, with long tubes, violently eruptive; and a fourth class, old and indisposed to eruption, unless angered by throwing stones down their throats. His theory of a geyser in action is summarized as follows: Suppose a geyser to have a simple but irregular tube, without a cave, in which the water is heated by volcanic fires or ejections. The water in this tube, being hotter the deeper it lies, reaches the boiling point somewhere below. The column of water in the tube is augmented by the flow from tributary hot springs at different levels beneath the surface, until at length the pressure is sufficiently great to generate steam far down below. This steam, in its effort to escape, at first forces up the water in the tube until it overflows the basin at the surface. By means of this overflow the pressure in every part of the tube is diminished; but a large body of water, before very near the boiling point, is instantly converted into steam, which rushes upward through the tube, projecting the column of water which has confined it high into the air. With this water a large volume of steam is also carried off; but the steam continues to escape from the tube some time after the water is exhausted. The premonitory rumblings before an eruption are only a simmering of the water on a great scale.

Rates for Special Conveyances, Etc.

Where regular conveyances are detained at the request of tourists holding the $35.00, $40.00 or $110.00 tickets, an extra charge will be made, as follows:

For two-horse carriage and driver, accommodating three people, $10.00 per day.

For four-horse carriage and driver, accommodating five people, $15.00 per day.

For four-horse carriage and driver, accommodating seven people, $20.00 per day.

The following are open tariff rates where persons desire to travel by special conveyances without using any of the several forms of tickets on sale at the offices of the N. P. R. R.:

For two-horse carriage and driver, accommodating three people, $14.00 per day.

For four-horse carriage and driver, accommodating five people, $18.00 per day.

For four-horse carriage and driver, accommodating seven people, $25.00 per day.

For one saddle horse or pony, $2.50 per day.

For one pack horse, $1.50 per day.

For one guide with his own saddle horse, $5.00 per day.

Ponies and saddle horses can be had at Mammoth Hot Springs, Grand Canon and Upper Geyser Basin.

Where carriage and saddle horses are desired for local use around Mammoth Hot Springs, Upper Geyser Basin and Grand Canon they can be obtained at the following prices:

For two-horse carriage and driver, accommodating three people, $4.00 first hour; $2.00 each subsequent hour; or $10.00 per day.

For one saddle horse or pony, $1.00 first hour; 50 cents each subsequent hour; or $2.50 per day.

Horses, (saddle or carriage,) without reference to ownership so long as they are being used by tourists, will be furnished feed and care at the different stables of the Transportation Company at reasonable rates provided the accommodations will permit.

Tourist's Memoranda.

TOURIST'S MEMORANDA.

May	June	July	August	September
		Sunday	18	

Monday 18

TOURIST'S MEMORANDA.

May   June   July   August   September

Tuesday   **18**

Wednesday   **18**

TOURIST'S MEMORANDA.

May　　*June*　　*July*　　*August*　　*September*

　　　　　　　Thursday　　18

　　　　　　　Friday　　18

TOURIST'S MEMORANDA.

May	*June*	*July*	*August*	*September*
		Saturday	18	
		Sunday	18	

TOURIST'S MEMORANDA.

May	June	July	August	September
		Monday	18

		Tuesday	18

TOURIST'S MEMORANDA.

May   June   July   August   September

Wednesday   *18*

Thursday   *18*

TOURIST'S MEMORANDA.

May	June	July	August	September
		Friday	18	

Saturday 18

TOURIST'S MEMORANDA.

May　　June　　July　　August　　September
　　　　　　　Sunday　　18

　　　　　　Monday　　15

TOURIST'S MEMORANDA.

May   June   July   August   September
Tuesday   18

Wednesday   18

TOURIST'S MEMORANDA.

May   June   July   August   September

Thursday   18

Friday   18

TOURIST'S MEMORANDA.

May   June   July   August   September

Saturday   18

Sunday   18

TOURIST'S MEMORANDA.

May	June	July	August	September
		Monday	18	
		Tuesday	18	

TOURIST'S MEMORANDA.

May   June   July   August   September
                Wednesday   18

                Thursday   18

TOURIST'S MEMORANDA.

May　　　June　　　July　　　August　　　September

　　　　　　　　　　Friday　　　　18

　　　　　　　　　　Saturday　　　18